LAUGHING
IN THE HILLS

LAUGHING IN THE HILLS

A Season at the Racetrack

BILL BARICH

Skyhorse Publishing

10 9 8 7 6 5 4 3 2 1

Library of Congress Cataloging-in-Publication Data is available on file.

Cover design by Jane Sheppard
Cover image: *Racehorses Before the Grandstand*, Edgar Degas

Print ISBN: 978-1-63450-551-2
Ebook ISBN: 978-1-63450-948-0

Printed in the United States of America

for Diana, *pazienza,*
and for my father

LAUGHING
IN THE HILLS

Chapter One

For me it did not begin with the horses. They came later, after a phone call and a simple statement of fact: *Your mother has cancer.* I remember the flight from California to New York, mountains giving way to flatlands, the sense of slippage I had. On Long Island the lawns were brittle with frost. "You won't recognize her," my father said. He was right. Disease had made her an old woman with bright eyes. She looked shrunken and tired. She'd made herself up for my arrival, with rouge, powder, and lipstick, and wore a new blue pants suit, but she'd bought it months ago and it served only to accentuate her boniness. What I felt in her fingers as she took my hand was a powerful desire to hold on.

In spite of her pain, she was a good patient, easy to be around. I never saw her openly sad. For the most part she sat very still in a lounge chair padded with pillows, reading or listening to the radio. She complained, joking, that her book, a thick hardback, was too heavy to support, that it kept slipping from her hands, and she worried about her family and her garden and rosebushes and all that she'd miss in the future if her chemotherapy treatments failed. On fine days she liked to sit outside bundled in sweaters and coats and take the sun on her face. She was like a passenger on a cruise ship just taking the sun. It was odd to see her becoming tanned and healthy-looking even as the cancer progressed.

There was nothing we could do to help. She was isolated within the disease and it consumed most of her energies. So we lost ourselves in mindless tasks, sweeping, cleaning, raking over the dead grass in the yard, but these gestures of avoidance were only partially successful. The truth kept ambushing us time and again, striking at all the wrong moments, bringing tears to our eyes. To escape it, I went for walks or borrowed the car and drove around the old neighborhood, through a summation of my youth, schools, playgrounds, baseball fields, longing in a not-so-curious way for the imperial symmetry of diamonds, for innocence, for breath.

Out of this desperation I started playing the horses. It happened quite suddenly. One afternoon I passed an Off-Track Betting office and stopped in and made a bet for fun, and the next thing I knew I was driving to the local newsstand every morning to buy the *Daily Racing Form,* an indispensable publication that gives a compact symbolic history of the horses entered in the day's races at major racetracks nearby. Beginners often find the *Form* overwhelming, since it offers more information than anybody could possibly absorb, including a horse's age, sex, color, parentage, birthplace, breeder, owner, trainer, racing record over the past two years, amount of money won, and so on, but most serious gamblers won't make a wager without first studying its contents.

At home I spread the *Form* on the kitchen table and began the perilous exercise known as handicapping, which involves weighing the merits and defects of all the entrants in a given race over and over again until the apparent winner emerges. The most telling facts were to be found in the past performance charts: blocks of statistics, one per horse, that showed in copious detail just how well that horse had done in its most recent outings, exactly where it had been positioned during four different phases (first quarter, half, stretch, and finish) of each race—called the running line—the caliber of competition it had been facing, its relative speed and preferred distance, along with several other factors essential to the handicapping process. I had studied the *Form* before but never with such intensity; now I bent to the charts like an adept parsing mystical texts. Sometimes they were runic, impossible to decipher, but other times winners stepped readily forward to speak their names.

When I finished handicapping I went to the OTB office to fill out my betting slips. I liked to watch people come in and slowly erode the antisepsis of the place, jabbing wet cigar butts into polished ashtrays and dragging muddy boots over clean tile floors. They were intent, blind to their surroundings, and they all looked terrific, at least until the first race had gone off. Optimism put a bloom in every cheek. Anything might happen, could happen, probably *would* happen, that was the notion being entertained at OTB. If you hit the triple, you might walk out the door a millionaire, your pockets larded with greenbacks. Even the fat man, who was otherwise shrewd, believed this. I met him one afternoon when he squeezed in next to me at the counter. He was so big his trousers had been split at the seam, then stretched out by the addition of an unmatching panel of cloth. He had diabetes, he said, and a bum ticker about to burst, and he'd been holed up at his sister's house in Hempstead since Thanksgiving. His own home was in Des Moines, but he couldn't bring himself to go back there. "No OTB in Iowa," he said, and I knew exactly what he meant.

3

It surprised me when everybody else in my family wanted to escape, too, including my mother. She always qualified her participation by saying that gambling was wrong, and played a few horses only, usually favorites, and my visiting aunt did the same, although she could be swayed by a name that recalled a pleasant memory or proposed a condition she sought, Happy Birthday or Long Vacation. My father, a lavish spender, bet every race, double, triple, and exactas as well, over-extended and incautious, while my brother played hunches, dark horses from his dreams, Obliterator, twenty on the nose. My sister never bet at all, but sometimes she joined us when we gathered on the porch every thirty minutes or so to listen to the delayed broadcast of the races. My mother would lean forward in her chair, her big reading glasses dwarfing her eyes, making them look childlike, and act excited if her horse was in contention. She had a funny way of exaggerating her response, pressing a fist to her sternum. My father said the races were good for her, they gave her something to look forward to. I thought she heard in the track announcer's call a little pulse of life at the heart of the cancer.

II

Back home in California I fell into a lingering sadness. There were miscarriages and more cancers among relatives, and then my wife was operated on for a brain tumor, which proved not to exist except as a dark spot on an X-ray plate. I tried to relax, reminding myself that worse things could have happened, but this was only intermittently useful. Tolerance was not the issue. In the autumn I quit my job and we moved to the country, to a battered trailer overlooking a river. For a while the isolation with its perishable sounds, herons, flowing water, the soft flutter of bugs born into the evening light, worked wonders, but then

4

I began to falter. Winter came and the money we'd saved was running out, and the things I wanted to write about remained just out of reach. I argued with my wife and she argued with me; we were older and childless and knee-deep in ruin.

Most afternoons I took long drives through the countryside, playing the radio loud and drinking cans of Brown Derby beer. I stopped in small towns with flags and libraries and looked for history in their thrift shops. In Cloverdale I found ashtrays shaped like oranges and lemons, souvenirs of the Citrus Fair; in Hopland part of a grape press; in Geyserville three handtowels from a razed hotel. These items were precious to me, shards of a human past that was being scraped from the edges of consciousness. All over the county, town houses and condominiums were devouring orchards and vineyards just as they'd devoured the potato farms on Long Island, and whenever I saw a sign for a new subdivision, Eternal Now Villas, Cypress Estates where no cypresses had ever grown, or read about the Corps of Engineers' plan to dam the river, or saw bulldozers or sewer pipes or even surveyors, I flew into a rage. The assault was relentless, without purpose, another aspect of disease.

Sometimes instead of driving I forded the river and hiked through the oaks and madrones of a sheep ranch nearby. I found the skull there, hidden in Spanish moss. It was small and dry, worn away in spots, and I could peel away its tissuelike layers with my fingers. I thought it might have belonged to a coyote, but a friend checked the dentition and said it was more likely a sheep's skull. Maybe a coyote had killed the sheep, he said, but if so the coyote was long gone and ghostly, laughing in the hills.

III

In the spring I felt no better. I wanted to forget about what had happened, what was happening, but I'd wake at night to my mother's face or the memory of my wife lying in her hospital bed, crying and outraged, while across the room an old lady who looked just like Auden in drag smoked Chesterfields and spoke favorably of the removal of her pituitary gland many years ago. The mix was weird and frightening and it came always at night, out of the deepest places. I began once again to long for an escape into orderliness and decided, with the same hapless illogic that governed all my actions then, to leave home and spend the rest of the spring at Golden Gate Fields, a thoroughbred track in Albany, near Oakland and San Francisco. There were other things I might have done, friends who would have taken me in, but I was convinced there was something special about racing and I wanted to get to the heart of the matter. The track seemed circumscribed and manageable, especially when compared to the complex filigree of nature, hydrogen intertwined with embryos and tumors. I kept thinking about the fat man and the pulse I'd first heard beating on Long Island. I thought if I could touch it, I might come away renewed.

IV

Once before I'd done something similar, when I was much younger but equally distraught. I'd escaped to Italy as a member of a college study group, but soon after arriving in Florence I started wandering instead of studying. The Renaissance became more immanent than historical to me and for six months I lived within its compass. I felt like a prince of existence; there were days when nothing at all went wrong. The city was mine and I explored it with a vengeance, leaving the Marchesa's apartment at dawn, a hard roll stuffed in my pocket and light just breaking over the Piazza della Signoria. I came to know the galleries of the Uffizi by heart, and the statuary along the Loggia dei Lanzi, and I could count to twenty in Italian and liked nothing better

6

than to sit at a café table and drink wine and read poetry or the queer striving philosophy of the Humanists, that loose-knit group of scholars who'd formed around the Medici. Pico della Mirandola was my favorite, Pico with his lumpy nose and straw-colored hair. It was said he'd been born with an aura around his head, bright as a candle flame, which meant he'd do great things but die early, in the time of lilies. He believed our position in the universal scheme was not fixed but fluid. "Thou, constrained by no limits, in accordance wtih thy own free will . . . shalt ordain for thyself the limits of thy nature." Such statements, however naive, had currency for me again, and when I came across a book of Pico's on my shelf I tossed it into the suitcase, then added Ficino, the Platonist, and Burckhardt, the historian, and some more general books about the Renaissance. Florentines, I thought, had always liked to gamble.

V

In Albany I had difficulty finding a place to stay. There were a few motels near the track, but their managers seemed to live in perpetual fear of guests. One lady spoke to me through a round metal speaker set into a shield of Plexiglas. Her voice had the absolute timbre of creaking hinges. "We're all full," she said, but her VACANCY sign was still blinking when I drove off. I wondered if the strangeness I felt at entering an alien environment, the suburbs, could already show so clearly in my face. At the next motel I rang the bell five times but nobody answered. When I looked through the office window, I saw an old man reclining in a lounger, his paper open to the racing page. At last I found a dilapidated corner house over the border in Richmond and rented a one-room apartment by the week. The landlady, an Okie named Mabel, made me sign a lease that effectively deprived me of all my rights. The room had no shower, only a tub, but if I

7

crouched low under the eaves near a front window I could watch the accidents along San Pablo Avenue. I spread my books, charts, and *Forms* over a small table and staked a psychic claim to the space, which was worn and lonely, a distillate of frailties.

That night my neighbor across the hall threatened to kill his wife. "Bitch!" he yelled. "You always making me feel so bad. Sit around all day smoking stuff while I got to work. How you think I like it, bitch?" Something broke, a glass or maybe a mirror. I kept waiting for bullets, but the argument had played before, many times; the actors were perfectly rehearsed and fell by degrees into a call-and-response routine that ended in tears and screams and the wife's frantic exit down the stairs. When I checked out in the morning, breaking my "lease," I could still smell her perfume, deeply floral, all along the hallway.

Finally I settled in at the Terrace Motel, a decent place with friendly owners, clean rooms, three-legged chairs propped against the walls, and a swimming pool. I never saw anybody in that pool, not once. The Terrace's population was constantly shifting, except for an Indian who wore his hair in braids and lived in one unit, and a few track employees and old people who rented minimally functional apartments in a building adjacent to the main motel. On warm evenings, just at twilight, somebody there played songs like "To Dream the Impossible Dream" on a very percussive piano. The boss maid had worked as a maid for eighteen years, and she told me she was ready for a vacation. "I'm not kidding you," she said. "I'd go just about anywhere." One morning I thought I saw Jimmy Cuzick, an apprentice jockey, walking barefooted across the parking lot, a patch over one eye. Cuzick had suffered a mild concussion days before when his mount, Spiced Falcon, a rogue shipper from Santa Anita, had thrown him in the starting gate, and I wanted to ask him about it, but when I came back from the races he was gone. This happened often around the track, people vanishing, positioning themselves at the proper angle to achieve invisibility. Horses sometimes vanished, too, but more often they just broke loose into new realms of the unexpected.

I hated nights at the Terrace. All the television sets came on, seemingly in unison, and the sound of them was unavoidable and rose around me like granite. I felt imprisoned in an aspect of the Middle Ages, some dark and barbarous time. The TVs spoke of cultural decay, of flattened perceptions and a cathodal substratum too insubstantial to support human life. Throughout the state, the spirit was being stripped of its tools for enrichment. Schools, libraries, and museums were closing, and citizens everywhere were retreating into the feudal dimensions of artificial light.

VI

In those blue waking hours I read about horses and racing and the Renaissance. I thought about aspirations, green shoots fibrillating in the concentricities of civilization. I thought about change.

Niccolò Machiavelli, in exile at his small farm above Florence, dressed in robes of office after nightfall, then went to his study and talked to the ancients. "I am not ashamed to speak with them," he wrote, "and ask them the reasons of their actions, and they, because of their humanity, answer me. Four hours can pass, and I feel no weariness; my troubles forgotten, I neither fear poverty nor dread death."

This too was what I wanted, to get past the sadness, but I remembered the first days of our family betting and how my aunt had played Little Miracle to win. The horse came in, surprising us all, and my mother died in the spring.

Chapter Two

Point Fleming, the site of Golden Gate Fields, is a rocky outcropping of land that extends into the eastern portion of San Francisco Bay. It was once occupied by a tribe of Indians known as Costonoans, from the Spanish for *coast peoples,* members of the Penutian language family. Costonoans lived in tule huts along the littoral and made an unfavorable impression on the padres who served as diarists for the early explorers. By all accounts they were an apathetic humorless tattooed band who did their best to avoid eye contact of any kind. They scalped their enemies, severing heads, then displaying them on poles, and ran around naked except in winter, when they put on odoriferous rabbit-skin blankets against the cold. They weren't very good at any of the traditional Indian skills, not basketry, hunting, or fishing. Sometimes they managed to knock a passing duck out of the sky or kill a deer with an obsidian-tipped arrow, but more often they subsisted on acorns scavenged from inland slopes and canyons, clams, mussels, and the few salmon they caught in their long unwieldy nets. These salmon were dispatched with vehemence. "Once I counted fifteen-odd blows and in another case twenty-odd," one diarist noted. The Costonoans also liked to gamble. They played *tussi,* a variety of guessing game, and may have learned a primitive version of craps from neighboring Yokuts women. Maybe the rattling of black walnut dice inhibited their ritual life, for the anthropologist Kroeber listed only one Costonoan dance song in his tribal compendium. It consists of a single lyric line repeated over and over again until an arbitrary ending is reached:

> *Dancing on the brink of the world*
> *Dancing on the brink of the world*
> *Dancing on the brink of the world*

II

In 1879 the Giant Powder Company, manufacturers and suppliers of dynamite, nitroglycerine, and blasting powder to gold miners, relocated to Point Fleming after an accident at their San Francisco plant had nearly leveled that city. Six months later their new plant exploded for the first time, killing eleven whites and twelve Chinese, but it was rebuilt immediately "due to the large number of orders on hand." Giant exploded next in 1883, terminating Superintendent Ferdinand Kampf and thirty-seven Chinese; then it merged with the Judson and Sheppard Chemical Works, only to explode twice more in 1892, blowing a boy through the roof, a man into the Bay, and three whites and two Chinese to Kingdom Come. Shock waves from the blast were felt a hundred miles away in Sacramento. The plant, left in ashes and rubble, turned into a tourist attraction, and special sheriff's deputies were appointed to keep the crowds under control.

III

The Point, with one red brick remnant at its tip, became a popular spot for swimming, picnicking, fishing, and boating. There were still a few clams and mussels to be dug in the shoals, and a

Chinaman paid cash on the line for every shark delivered to his shack. A caretaker lived in a house near the old powder works bridge and grew corn and potatoes near the marshes. He hauled his produce to market in a dray wagon pulled by two gray horses. When his wife died, he was left alone on the Point, an antiquated hermit, and committed suicide by sticking his head into a barrel of drinking water and swimming upstream into memory.

In 1908 the township east of the Point, numbering about two hundred people, voted to incorporate as Ocean View. A year later the residents had second thoughts, and in a special election changed Ocean View to Albany, honoring their mayor, Frank Roberts, a native of Albany, New York. Albany's subsequent growth was rapid: 1,500 by 1913, 2,350 by 1918, progressing by stucco and plaster spurts until the area was packed densely with bungalows, cottages, and two-story apartments. Now the city has a population of roughly fifteen thousand and exists as a kind of buffer zone between working-class Richmond and the congestive liberalism of Berkeley. Shiny new police cars cruise the boulevards, suggesting a state of siege; forty-eight cents of every city dollar are budgeted for public safety, none for public health. In 1978 the central civic phenomenon seemed to be the Battle of the Burgers. It was occurring everywhere, but the skirmishes were concentrated most heavily along San Pablo Avenue. Franchises had fired the opening salvo, quarter-pound hamburgers, into the market economy, and now the owners of older independent drive-ins were massing a counterattack. Their windows were covered with hastily lettered signs taped up among fading photos of milkshakes, happy tots, and corndogs fully erect. OUR BURGERS GUARANTEED ONE-THIRD POUND, the signs declared, and the effect was devastating.

IV

In 1940 a group of investors decided to build a racetrack, The Albany Turf Club, on Point Fleming. Maury Diggs, architect, and Jack Casson, general contractor, were in charge of the project. Their plant design had many virtues, not the least of which was a grandstand located on a hill above the Bay, but the racing strip itself, so central to the scheme of things, proved to be their downfall. Racing strips are always difficult to construct, requiring a specialized knowledge of agronomy, and in Albany the job was further complicated by coastal fog, punishing seasonal rains, and the softening effects of Bay tides on the subsoil. Unfortunately for Diggs and Casson, the winter of 1940–41 was a particularly rough one. The Turf Club was scheduled to open on New Year's Day, but the strip was so muddy and potholed by then that management kept postponing the ·date, hoping for a break in the weather. It never came. Rain fell through most of January, and finally, with creditors pressuring them, the group was forced to open early in February. The strip had partially dissolved, rivulets cracked its surface everywhere, and it was not uncommon for horses in the starting gate to sink up to their knees in the muck. The abbreviated meet ended four days later when a horse went down so horribly, breaking a leg in half, that the track was obliged to close. Bankruptcy proceedings followed. The Santa Fe Railroad, from whom the land on the Point had been leased, acquired the plant and subsequently loaned it to the U.S. Navy for use as a training base after the Japanese bombed Pearl Harbor. Barns were fitted with plywood panels and turned into barracks, the infield was stacked high with amphibious gear and LST boats, and tight-lipped boys from the Midwest learned to read a radar screen while cruising the Bay just off the backstretch.

V

The Turf Club, under new management and now named Golden Gate Fields, opened again in 1947 with a considerably improved racing strip. The principal component was sandy loam from Antioch, which held together well even under downpours and tidal fluctuations. When the sun shone and the wind blew, the reconstituted strip became so hard, dry, and fast that even knob-kneed platers looked good. Six world records were set in just a few years, two on the same afternoon, October 4, 1947, when Fair Truckle went six furlongs in 1:08 ⅖ and Count Speed covered a mile and a sixteenth in 1:41. Bill Shoemaker broke his maiden at Golden Gate in 1949 aboard Shafter V, and Johnny Longden made frequent appearances, winning nine of the first twenty Golden Gate Handicaps, including the inaugural on Fred Astaire's Triplicate. The Calumet Special used to roll into the Albany railroad station direct from Kentucky and debouch a priceless cargo of thoroughbreds, who were then led to the barns via an old slaughterhouse tunnel that ran beneath the freeway. In 1950 Citation, Calumet's pride, established a new world record for the mile, 1:33⅗, and later in the meeting confronted Charles Howard's Noor in two classic races. Noor had beaten Citation twice at Santa Anita, and he did it twice more up north despite carrying heavy weight in the last outing.

In 1957 Silky Sullivan made his debut at Golden Gate and introduced his penchant for late-breaking finishes. Silky became a national hero, the underdog in apotheosis, by lagging far behind the field until the stretch, looking uninterested, then shifting into overdrive and passing other horses as though they were mired in the recollected muck of Turf Club days. He boosted attendance at the track, but he wasn't bred for superstardom. His bloodlines unraveled in the Kentucky Derby—he finished out of the money, distanced—and things were never quite the same again. Silky's voluminous mail, from kids, teachers, innocents, and a few other gentle souls who thought he could read as well as run, was forwarded to a farm in Napa where he stood at stud. Every year on St. Patrick's Day, he was vanned to the track and paraded past the grandstand, often pausing to kick up his heels, until he died in his sleep of a heart attack in 1978 at the age of twenty-two. He was buried in the infield, his grave marked by a white picket fence, its borders enlivened by multicolored violas.

Shortly after Silky's retirement, the California Horse Racing Board, the body that governs racing in the state, precipitated the demise of first-class racing in northern California by discontinuing its practice of assigning exclusive dates for racing meetings. Before 1964 the Board had permitted only one major thoroughbred track in the state to be open at any given time; Santa Anita and Hollywood Park were dark while Golden Gate was running. But racing associations, the corporate bodies that operate and sometimes own racetracks, were lobbying for a more liberal arrangement—simultaneous meetings and overlapping dates—in hopes of increasing profits, and the Board finally acquiesced. Soon thereafter the southern California tracks, wealthier than their northern counterparts and drawing on a larger population, began offering bigger purses and better facilities and soon cornered the market on prime thoroughbred flesh. The quality of stock performing in the north declined steadily, and Golden Gate devolved to its present state of repair, an elegantly situated, slightly rundown plant featuring indifferent and often curious racing early in the week and more bettable affairs toward the weekend.

Today, Golden Gate encompasses 225 acres, with stalls for 1,425 horses, seats for 13,004 humans, and enough space overall to cram in a crowd of 30,000, although no such crowd has materialized of late. In 1978 the daily attendance averaged 9,429, down eight percent from the previous year, while the handle remained firm at about $1,450,000. The average fan wagered $160 every time through the turnstiles. Two separate racing associations, Pacific and Tanforan, sponsor meetings at the track. The Pacific meet usually begins in late January and runs through mid-April; Tanforan, always of shorter duration, ends early in June. Between them, the associations distribute purses totaling $7,000,000 over 98 racing days. The grandstand at Golden Gate, like grandstands everywhere, is divided into levels connotative of social class: General Admission, Clubhouse, Turf Club, and the exclusive Directors' Club, a glassed-in box right over the finish line where the track's directors and their guests can eat, drink, and wager without plebeian interference. To the left of the Club, just beyond the executive offices, is a penthouse apartment reserved for special friends of the management. Rumor has it that Jimmy Durante once spent a honeymoon there, but nobody seems to know whether he won or lost. Looking up from the paddock where the horses are saddled you can see the penthouse curtains just above the wide tinted windows of the press box. Fans sitting in the grandstand proper miss the sight of curtains but are treated on windy days to something equally mysterious, the smell of salt borne inland from unseen waters.

VI

The night before the meet began, I sat at my unconventionally four-legged Terrace desk and prepared to handicap the following day's races. I had no system or standard approach, but there were a few things I always took into account before making a tentative selection: *speed,* which could be gauged in general fashion from a horse's recent running times; *class,* which was a function both of breeding and the level (races were ranked by the size of the purse offered, handicap first, then stakes, allowance, and claiming) at which a horse had been competing; and *condition,* which meant fitness and was expressed by a horse's recent finishes (if they were good or improving, the horse was said to be "on form") and its showing during the daily exercise period, morning workouts (recent workout times were given at the bottom of each horse's chart). The trainer and jockey associated with a horse also affected my decision. Certain trainers were downright inept and never won a race regardless of their stock, and not a few riders at Golden Gate were incapable of handling their mounts.

I also considered post position as a potential factor in the outcome of a race. Before leaving home I'd compiled a post-position survey of races run during the Pacific meeting that was just ending. I'd done this to see if there was an advantage to be gained by breaking from a particular post (the slot a horse is assigned in the starting gate; there are rarely more than twelve horses entered in a race), and to determine whether front-runners, horses who broke quickly, took the lead, and tried to hold it throughout (going *wire-to-wire*) fared better at Golden Gate than one would expect. The survey proved instructive. In races over a mile, called *routes,* the outside posts, seven through twelve, were as disadvantageous as usual; horses stuck out there had more ground to cover. In races under a mile, called *sprints,* the survey turned up a surprise. Ordinarily, the best posts in a short race are those closest to the rail, but during the Pacific meet horses starting near the middle of the track, posts four and five, had won more often than horses inside them. Furthermore, horses breaking from the seven slot had won almost as often as those breaking from the one slot. The survey indicated as well that front-runners won over thirty percent of all sprints at Golden Gate. Facts like these were invaluable when trying to choose between two otherwise closely matched thoroughbreds.

As an additional edge I'd brought along three books on handicapping technique: Tom Ainslie's *Complete Guide to Thoroughbred Racing,* Andy Beyer's *Picking Winners,* and Steve Davidowitz's *Betting Thoroughbreds.* These books were not typical of the genre; most handicapping tracts are lurid affairs that sucker readers into parting with a few dollars in exchange for an easy-to-follow system guaranteed to produce eight million dollars in just three short weeks. Ainslie, Beyer, and Davidowitz were serious, intelligent men who never underestimated the complexity of the sport. Ainslie was the dean of the company. His book was the most informative about all aspects of racing and is still the best primer around. He favored a balanced approach to making a selection, weighing all the factors much as I had been doing.

Beyer was more dogmatic. As an undergraduate at Harvard he'd gotten hooked on racing and had since "perfected" a system based on the digital-computer research of Sheldon Kovitz, a fellow student and doctoral candidate in mathematics. Apparently, Kovitz was too busy feeding numbers into his IBM 360 Model 40 to succeed himself, but Beyer saw in his calculations the seed of Something Big, a way to incorporate relativity into speed ratings. Most ratings, like those given in the *Form,* were suspect because they were derived from nonexistent absolutes. A horse who'd earned an 80 on Tuesday was not *exactly* as fast as a horse who'd earned an 80 on Wednesday because the track surface changed every day (or even from moment to moment), and Tuesday's conditions were always different from Wednesday's —faster or slower by critical fractions. Beyer adopted Kovitz's method, improved it, and parlayed the results into a complicated mathematical system. It was the best in the world, he claimed.

"Speed figures are the way, the truth and the light," wrote Beyer. "And my method of speed handicapping is, I believe, without equal."

I found Davidowitz's book the most pithy and available. He seemed a little tougher than the other men, more hard-nosed, and it showed in his jacket photo. While Ainslie looked like a businessman and Beyer like a computer programmer with a side interest in recreational drugs, Davidowitz looked mean. His face had a demonic cast; an eyebrow was arched in perpetual scrutiny. I liked the knack he had for making direct, incontrovertible statements: *When a three-year-old is assigned actual top weight in a race for horses three years and up, the three-year-old has little or no chance of winning*. Such gems were inlaid throughout the text, always supported by statistics. Davidowitz further endeared himself by being quick to point a finger at the criminal element in racing whenever he encountered it. Most turf writers were unwilling to print anything but bland idealizations of the sport.

After skimming through the books, I put all the materials aside and reached into my pocket, as I'd been doing every hour or so since leaving home. Again I counted my money—five hundred dollars in twenty-dollar bills. It looked pitiful stacked on the desk, the smallest stake any would-be gambler ever started with. I felt embarrassed. I thought the stake was correlated directly with my life: impoverished spirit, empty wallet. Such stupid flashes of guilt often overtook me after midnight. I tried to ignore this one, though, and took a shower and went to bed.

VII

Early the next morning, April 19, the first morning of Tanforan, I went to Golden Gate Fields ready to win. The grandstand was empty and quiet, with the cool feel of an aluminum mixing bowl waiting for ingredients. The sun climbed slowly over the eucalyptus trees on Albany Hill, huge blue gums planted there a century ago to shield the town from the reports of Industry on the Point. From the clubhouse rail I could see the backstretch and the neat rows of wooden barns and the soiled straw piled high at the corners of the rows. The hotwalking machines were turning. They were a recent addition to the track and had made obsolete a job grooms used to do, walking horses until they'd cooled down after exercising. There was a power pack at the base of each machine, and from it rose a thin shaft with four metal arms arranged in the shape of a cross. The arms were about six feet long and resembled in their positioning the blades of a propeller. When the power was on, the shaft revolved slowly and the horses, hitched by their halters to insulated cords dangling from the arms, were forced to circle until their pulse rates dropped and their breathing was not so labored. As they circled they looked like flywheels turning within the greater geometry of the backstretch, suggesting an intricate timepiece thrown open to bits of biology.

I took the escalator to the ground floor and walked through the paddock area. The green wear-forever carpet was worn thin, the railings were chipped and needed paint, and the saddling stalls, green and white, were scarred with half-moons incised by hoofs. The Par Three course laid out on the infield grass was soon to be closed for lack of patronage, but an OPEN sign hung in the pro shop window. I saw my face reflected among irons sticking out of a plaid bag. House sparrows pecked at seeds the harrow had uncovered, hopping around among the horse apples. The turf course surprised me. It was rough and stubby, spiked with crabgrass and not nearly as smooth as it looked from above. Two redwing blackbirds were mating in the caked mud of a drainage ditch. The male's epaulets were scarlet, brilliantly exposed as he drew his lover into a caped embrace.

Near the winner's circle I found a monument to Silky Sullivan.

It was built of bricks and mortar and looked like the chimney of a backyard barbecue pit. A bronze plaque was set into the center of the chimney, and on it was inscribed a celebratory poem written by Elaine Marfoglia of Pasadena.

Out of the gate like a bullet of red,
Dropping behind as the rest speed ahead,
Loping along as the clubhouse fans cheer,
Leisurely stalking the field in first gear.

Down the backstretch forty lengths far behind,
Unconcerned—strictly the following kind;
Muscles in motion, nostrils aflare,
Holding the pace with a casual air.

The poem continued for a few more stanzas, then galloped toward a finish as heart-tugging as any of Silky's.

And now he's at rest, where all champions go;
We'll miss the parade of his "Derby Day" show.
As he pranced and kicked up his heels for the crowd,
He was loved—he was big, he was gentle and proud.

About eleven-thirty fans began arriving in steady streams, and as I watched them come in I had the sense of a jointly imagined form evolving, something entirely apart from horses and jockeys. Each person seemed to carry a narrative element in his head, and these elements were being woven gradually into the prevailing fiction. It was modeled on notions of symmetry and coherence. The electronic devices around the track reinforced the fiction in the warm-up patterns they flashed: the infield toteboard showed four rows of zeros balanced one on top of another, the smaller totes inside offered odds of five to five at every slot, and the closed-circuit TVs featured tiny dots boxed at perfect intervals within a neatly squared grid. The gift shop lady displayed her horsehead bookends in a horseshoe-shaped arc, and the popcorn lady, her striped smock in harmony with the trim of her booth, checked to see that the empty cardboard boxes she would later fill were distributed in evenly matched stacks. The fiction was carefully, if unconsciously, projected and didn't begin to dissipate until the National Anthem had been played and the horses came sauntering up from the barns in single file. Then order gave way to chaos.

VIII

The moment when horses enter the paddock before a race can be a bad one. Statistics that had earlier seemed so definitive are translated peremptorily into flesh, and flesh is heir to miseries, bandaged legs, a limp, a nervous froth bubbling on a filly's inner thighs. Many times I've heard people groan when they saw what their figures had led them to, some scarred creature with downcast eyes. I was fortunate on the opening day of Tanforan. The horse I'd chosen at the Terrace, Southern Gospel, looked good. He was a rangy chestnut gelding with a polish to his coat. He was breaking from the preferential four hole, too, which should have set my mind at ease, but I was feeling anxious. I'd been away from the track for some time and my responses to its stimuli were heightened, exaggerated. Every flickering movement made an impression on me, and I tried to take them all into account. Suddenly other horses began looking good. Folklore's Lite, who'd earned a high Beyer speed rating, was up on his toes. When I opened the *Form* to compare him with Southern Gospel, I saw instead something I'd missed before, excellent workouts for Top Pass. Was Top Pass ready to make his bid?

Davidowitz might think so. The more I read, the more confused I became. The *Form* kept bursting open, punctured by discoveries, ruining my cartographic efforts.

Next I felt the concentrative energy of the bettors around me. They were staring at the paddock just as piercingly as I was, working hard to affect the outcome of the race. It was as though many versions of reality were competing for a chance to obtain. The man next to me was steaming. He wore the blissful expression of a monk in his tenth hour of *zazen;* smoke was about to issue from his ears. I stood there paralyzed, unable to make a choice. I was afraid that if I lost my first bet, a downward trend would be irreversibly established. With three minutes to go I ran to the windows and bet a horse I hadn't even considered before, Spicy Gift, because I'd noticed that he'd had some bad luck last time out, which indicated, absolutely, that he was bound, perhaps even *compelled,* to win. When I walked away I realized I'd just put ten bucks on a twenty-to-one shot. Handicapping overkill, the brain weaving useless webs. Spicy Gift finished somewhere in the middle of the field, beaten by Bargain Hostess, a filly and first-time starter who broke from the outermost post. These factors had eliminated her from contention in my mind; now I saw them for what they were, markers of talent.

But it was too late, I was locked into a loser's mind-set and couldn't shake free of it. All day long I compounded my mistakes, playing the most improbable nags on the card, hoping to get even, to start over, the slate wiped clean, Hong Kong Flew, Skinny Dink, throwing what little expertise I had out the window, Hey Mister M.A., a toad at fifty-seven to one, *giving* it away, then Queequeg in the eighth race because of Melville and what they'd found taped under his desk after he'd died, a scrap of paper on which he'd written, *Be true to the dreams of your youth;* but Queequeg drowned too, leaving me adrift, not even a coffin for support, and in the ninth, a broken man, I latched on to the favorite, Crazy Wallet, and watched in disgust as he hobbled home fifth. Down I went, spiraling, down and down, done in but good, sixty dollars fed irretrievably into the belly of the beast and still the breeze did blow.

IX

The whiskey at the Home Stretch bar was soothing, lucid, un-statistical, and I sipped it and stared at the photos on the back bar wall, pictures of horses and people and one large oil painting of Emmett Kelly, the clown, his bum hat wreathed in losing tickets. About seven o'clock a skinny man in a new denim leisure suit came in, accompanied by a short silent Mexican who looked as though he'd just eaten a shoe.

"Glad you're alive," the bartender said to the Mexican, grinning sarcastically. "You want more Cutty and Seven or'd you get enough last night?"

"Give him a beer," the other man said. "He doesn't need any Cutty. He was sick all over the barn this morning. Somebody else had to rub his horses. Isn't that right?"

The Mexican smiled happily and drank his beer.

A slim blond girl, barely out of her teens, was dancing with a man even smaller than the Mexican. He was jockey-size and had the powerful shoulders and arms that jockeys often develop. The blonde drank a beer as she danced, tipping back the bottle and closing her eyes. When the music ended she came over to the man in the leisure suit, pushed out her chest, and asked to borrow twenty dollars.

"I have three tickets I can cash in tomorrow," she said. "I've been holding on to them. As soon as I cash in, I'll pay you back."

"Honey," the man said, not unkindly, "that story has a beard."

She shrugged, looking unruffled, as though she made this pitch on a daily basis and expected a certain percentage of turndowns, and went back to the jockey-size man and asked him for five dollars. When he delivered, she used part of the money to buy a six-pack, then fed the jukebox and started dancing with yet another man, also very small, and when the music stopped this time she left with him, wiggling her compact hips.

"You ever see anybody who *needs* money forget to cash in?" the man asked. "No way. Does not happen. That girl loves jockeys. I think she might be a groupie."

The Home Stretch was often like this, friendly, wistful, and a little ragged at the edges. Grooms, trainers, winners, losers, mailmen, any and all of them were likely to wander in and sit down and order a drink and then tell you their life story, or at least the most immediate part of it, how they'd dropped a sawbuck on a Sure Thing only to see the horse go wide on the turn and wind up in the parking lot. The day bartender, Benny, a cigar-chomping five-by-fiver out of a Joe Palooka comic strip, ran the place with an iron hand and brooked no displays of unnecessary roughness. He yelled as loudly at friends as at enemies. "Whaddaya want? A Bud? Speak up. Can't *hear* you!" Once I heard somebody say to him, "Benny, like you to meet a friend of mine, he's a nice guy." Benny frowned. "We're *all* nice guys in here," he said. On the wall there was a photo of him and Rocky Marciano. Benny had his head on the Rock's shoulder and he was smiling like a baby. After dark, when the regulars disappeared, the Home Stretch underwent a subtle transformation. Drunken grooms began talking to themselves, and pale outsiders with unauthorized business to effect somewhere in the night sat alone and sipped iced gin, their eyes on the clock.

The man in the denim leisure suit, whose name was Sam Edwards, told me about his life. He worked for a trainer who worked in turn for a wealthy Indian, an India Indian, handling a string of forty horses. Sam supervised the trainer's grooms, most of them Mexicans, and was responsible for shipping the stock from track to track, Santa Anita to Golden Gate, then back again. He liked his job, but not the trainer—his methods were too "European"—and he looked forward to summertime, when the horses would again move east. He loved Saratoga for the partying and Belmont for the education he'd gotten there. Sometimes the vets had allowed him to descend along with them into a subterranean room where they performed autopsies on horses who'd died on the grounds. They did this for insurance purposes, to pinpoint the cause of death. There was a big difference, at least in the eyes of adjusters, between a mare who'd died of a heart attack and a mare who'd died of a heart attack while stoked on cocaine. One day a doctor showed Sam a torn stifle muscle on a dead horse's inner thigh and let him feel the separated flesh, and that same afternoon Sam diagnosed a similar complaint in a lame animal at his barn. The trainer he worked for then didn't believe him, of course, but that was how things went around the track. Sam left this trainer not much later, when the man refused to lend him money during a poker game.

"And I'd been with him for a couple of years," Sam said wearily. "I'll tell you, someday I'm going to retire. I got these two broodmares back on my grandmother's farm, they're both in foal right now. Maybe I'll get lucky this time. You never know for sure. Look at Seattle Slew. That horse wasn't bred to be a champion. I might win the Derby yet."

He ordered another round and drew faces in the frost of his beer glass. He'd told me earlier that he liked art. Whenever he visited a track he hadn't been to before, he saved a pari-mutuel ticket—every track issued different ones, with different colors and symbols—and when he retired he planned to paste them all together in a collage and hang it over his fireplace in the house he planned to buy.

"I love horses, you know. I think they must have eight senses instead of five. Like ESP. I *know* they have ESP. I had this one filly, she always washed out, got real nervous and sweaty before a thunderstorm. You could almost predict the weather by how washy she was."

"You think we have extra senses, too?"

"Could be," said Sam. "Could possibly be. Sometimes when I walk into a room I know I've been there before. I believe in reincarnation. I know I've had more than one life. When they made the planet, you know, there was only so much water created. It rains, the rain evaporates and goes back up in the clouds for next time. Same thing with people. Only so much people stuff to go around."

I asked him how he'd come to work with horses, and he said it went way back, to a particular grade school afternoon when the class bully had popped him one and raised a welt on his lip. Walking home he'd passed the neighborhood junkman (this was maybe forty years ago), and the junkman said, "Why you crying, son?" and led him into an alley where an old rundown junk-cart horse was tethered to a signpost. The horse was lathered and looked immense. "How'd you like to take a ride?" the junkman asked, and without waiting for an answer lifted Sam onto the horse's back and sent him sailing out into the full bright panorama of the street. Sam felt his troubles leaving, and the power of the horse rising up. This was the beginning, said Sam, "and I never did recover."

X

It was past midnight when I left the bar but I still wasn't ready to sleep. Back at the Terrace the TV sets would be tuned to Johnny Carson, and I wanted to avoid those emanations at all cost. Watching Carson robbed you of your essence, I thought. He occupied strange latitudes, flat plastic zones of the interior, and if you watched him long enough you could feel yourself oozing into the tubes and being sucked onto the set, where you became a part of Burbank, perhaps forever. It was even possible you might start wearing vinyl trousers and telling jokes about your mother-in-law. So instead of returning I drove across the railroad tracks to see what Golden Gate Fields looked like by night. Down by the rocks at the edge of the Bay somebody was fishing. He wore a black knit cap pulled low on his forehead, and he was whistling softly. A package of salted anchovies rested at his feet and moonlight caught in the crystals and blinked like charges of phosphorus at the tideline. I asked him what he was after.

"Striped bass," he said.

"Doing any good?"

"Nothing, man. I need some grass shrimp or something, some pileworms."

He worked as a groom and it wasn't bad work, he said, but the climate didn't agree with him and the fishing was strictly for amateurs. In the town where he'd grown up, near Mazatlán, even kids caught big snook, and he himself had nailed a black marlin in the Sea of Cortez when he was just fourteen. I told him about fishing for steelhead on the river at home and how they had the same lustrous quality as stripers, an opalescence shimmering on their scales. They were an anadromous species and lived most of their lives in salt water but returned unerringly to the fresh waters of their birth at spawning time. We knew where they chose to spawn, in creeks and estuaries, but I wondered if there was an equally distinct point deep in ocean waters that marked the other half of the egg.

I told the groom about the dam and how it would eventually

kill off the steelhead. He wanted to know why the dam was being built, and I said I didn't know, but of course I did. The dam would impound water to form an artificial lake, and the land around the lake would appreciate in value, and the realtors and developers would build the usual tacky resort facilities, and the people who made their fortunes by destroying things would be a little richer but not any safer from death. The dam was also a product of the zones Johnny Carson occupied, and of the current bias against historical modes of perception and the relevance of the past. But these matters were too disheartening to talk about after midnight on a losing day, so I gave the groom the last beer from my six-pack, wished him good luck, and drove away.

XI

In the Costonoan creation myth, all the world was water, and from this water two peaks rose, Mount Diablo and Reed's Peak. There were no humans, only Coyote, and Coyote was alone. Then one day from his place on the peak, Coyote saw a feather floating on the water. He watched the feather, and as he watched, it turned suddenly into a eagle, and Eagle flew up and joined Coyote on the peak. Coyote liked his new companion so much that they played together for a long time before even giving a thought to making any humans. Then they decided to make the Costonoans.

Chapter Three

In the morning I felt better. Morning is the best, the most optimistic, time at any racetrack; everything seems possible again. Some mornings when I left the Terrace early, just after six, to watch the horses working out, the dawn light filtering through the fog on the Bay echoed the gold I'd seen in painted halos all over Florence. I thought I could feel its healing properties. Out on the freeway the first commuters were tangling, but from where I stood along the rail I was aware only of the animals. Around me there rose the smells of manure, tobacco, coffee, and new-mown grass, and I found myself agreeing implicitly with Slaughterhouse Red, the gateman who supervised the comings and goings of riders, when he raised his abused face to the sun and said, "Anybody don't like *this* life is daffy!" Red was a former cowboy who'd grown up in the old Butchertown section of San Francisco and earned his keep as a boy by herding cattle from stockyard trains to the slaughterhouses lining the streets. He worked at the track until noon and then, if the weather was good, left for Martinez, where his fishing boat was docked. If the weather was only fair, or if an old buddy was in town, or even if he just had the itch, he stayed.

around for the afternoon's races. If the itch was bad, he'd been known to drive directly from Golden Gate to Bay Meadows so he could catch the quarterhorse races held there at night.

Horses came up from the barns in constant process, differing appreciably in their approach. Some looked half-awake, some looked sore, and some looked lazy. Some kicked up their heels because they were feeling good, while others, the rogues in need of stricter handling, bucked and snorted and let it be understood they were performing under duress. The true racehorses were always ready. They took to the track prancing, and when they returned from a gallop they were slick with sweat and their veins protruded in marmoreal splendor. A few of them wanted to keep right on running, and their riders were forced to hold them tight, pulling in on the reins, which put a crook into the horses' necks and gave them the look of knights on a chessboard. They were beautiful. Ponies and humans were interspersed among them, but they provided the movement, the exhilaration. Back at the barns they were bathed and brushed, then hooked to hotwalkers and set to circling. Everywhere I looked I saw horses, chestnuts, bays, browns, and blacks, and sometimes Gray Dandy or White Sprite, singularly elegant animals, and I felt locked within the clashing perspective of a battle scene painted by Paolo Uccello.

Right from the start horses move fast. A mare gives birth in fifteen to thirty minutes and after parturition her foal, born with eyes open, begins to pull away, tugging its legs out of the vagina and breaking the umbilical cord. In less than an hour, the foal is standing and looking around and in two hours can suckle, walk, vocalize, and show affection for its mother. Before the first day is out, the foal can trot, gallop, protect itself from insects by nipping, kicking, and shaking its tail, play, and even forage. Mares secrete mother's milk, colostrum, and it gives the foal antibodies and serves as a purgative. Even the digestive system of horses is geared to acceleration. They process food almost twice as fast as cows and can live on poor quality graze because their stomachs rapidly transform any available protein into amino acids. But they have to eat twice as much, twice as fast, and their teeth are sometimes worn down to the jawbone by the high silica content of grass. In the wild, toothless horses starve to death. Racehorses are fed hay and oats with an occasional taste of mash, a healthy balanced diet, but their relatives in other parts of the world exist on oddments like grapevines, lawn clippings, compost, bamboo leaves, and dried fish. Whatever they eat passes quickly through them. They defecate five to twelve times a day and urinate seven to eleven times. They have a normal body temperature of 100.3° Fahrenheit, which they maintain by shivering and sweating. The panniculus muscle beneath their skin allows them to shake off excess moisture, along with pesky flies, and acts as a thermostatic control.

But horses don't see very well. They are often astigmatic and suffer, too, from color blindness. To them the backstretch—the barn area behind the racing strip that also functions as a meeting ground and sometimes home for trainers, jockeys, grooms, and other track habitués—appears as a band of varying shades of gray, light differentiated. They don't register individual items like pails, hoses, or saddles, but they know when their groom is moving by changes in relative brightness and tone, the swath his figure cuts into the fixity of things. A horse's ears are concave and can move in any direction like dish antennae, picking up sounds at a great distance, a mouse scratching five stalls down. When a horse pricks its ears, its nostrils flare simultaneously, permitting the receptors to work in tandem. Stallions can smell a mare in heat miles away if she's upwind, and even an average horse can locate water and snakes by following its nose. Horses back off from strong-smelling substances, though, and have a curious inability to distinguish edible plants from poisonous ones. While I watched the horses come and go, business around me was booming. Jockeys' agents carrying small notebooks with hand-tooled leather covers moved from barn to barn booking mounts. If they represented a live rider, a kid who'd been winning lately, trainers met them eagerly and even offered them a cup of coffee, but if they were pushing a loser, their eyes were often sunk in rummy sadness and they were treated like pariahs. "Lemme know if you get something Richie can't handle," they shouted to Bob Hack, the agent who held Richie Galarsa's book, and Hack steered them on occasion to a needy trainer. Everybody wanted to use Galarsa because he was live, i.e., hot, and still had the bug, a five-pound weight allowance granted to apprentice riders, called bugboys, who hadn't yet won forty races. Some trainers thought the bug was more important than skill. If they couldn't have Richie, they'd ask for Enrique Muñoz, Hack's other boy, or try to corner Tony Diaz or Bill Mahorney or another of the handful of pros at Golden Gate who knew the difference between race-riding and just sitting on a horse's back and saying "Go." It was tough for middling-ability jocks like Art Lobato, who'd lost the bug and now spent mornings doing his own hustling, but it was even worse for those who clearly weren't going to make it. They stood near me at the rail, wearing caps stitched with their names, *Ed, Rodrigo, Julio,* and they were always solemn and moved their whips idly through the air. "Catch me a little later, I'm busy now," trainers shouted at them, disappearing into the cafeteria even as these jocks would later disappear, dropping through the levels of the track, Portland Meadows, Yakima Meadows, until they slipped at last into space.

Trainers had more important things to do than to mess with simpering jockeys. They had horses to clock, agents to contact, grooms to supervise, orders to place with tack salesmen and feed suppliers, and they had to be ready when the vet arrived to examine sick or damaged stock. And they had to waste precious time trying to read the Condition Book, which was about as cleanly written as an IRS pamphlet. The Condition Book set forth the eligibility requirements for future races, and it was updated every ten days. You needed a postgraduate degree to unscramble its sentences.

Starter Allowance, Purse $9,000, for four-year-olds and upward, non-winners of two races at one mile and one-eighth or over in 1978, which have started for a claiming price of $16,000 or less in 1977–78 and since that start have not won a race other than maiden or claiming or starter race exceeding $16,000.

Jay-sus! the trainers cried, dumping the book into an empty feed bucket. Most of them relied on agents when it came time to enter a horse. "Where do you think I ought to run ole Wind Chime?" they'd ask, and Hack or somebody else would set them straight, presenting the options.

Trainers (they were the first to tell you) had a rough job, even top guys like Bobby Martin and Bill Mastrangelo. Maybe Mastrangelo seemed relaxed when he walked around the barn singing Jerry Vale ballads at the top of his lungs, but he felt the pressure anyway. He had to feel it because he *had* to deal with owners, who applied it. Owners were almost always trouble. Sure, they looked classy when you saw them on TV at the Kentucky Derby, rich, polite, soft-spoken, but this image was deceiving. In fact they were part of the incomprehensible freeway universe, and ninety percent of them knew absolutely nothing, *nada,* zip, about horses or racing. Five of the remaining ten percent *thought* they knew something but didn't, and four of the final five percent were jerks with money to burn. They'd buy a rickety colt as a tax loss, and when the colt broke his maiden, finally winning his first race after sixteen tries, the jerks thought they owned another Man O' War and ordered the trainer to jump the colt to stakes races, where the competition was much tougher, and then when the colt lost repeatedly, by grotesque margins, they blamed the trainer or fired him or moved the colt to another track and skipped out on the balance of their bill. What could you do, take them to court? So trainers were to be forgiven, at least by other trainers, if at the end of workouts at ten, they left their stock in the care of grooms and ducked over to Spenger's for a few belts of confidence before the first race.

Inside the track cafeteria, a resonant humming of hot tips bounced off glass and Formica surfaces, and various intrepid characters huddled with their brokers, studying the day's program. All-night newsboys of indeterminate age distributed papers from pouches slung over their necks, looking a little like Hummel figurines. *Best chance play of race. Three-star special. Romero's best.* Discarded front page sections littered the floor, but you couldn't find a sports page anywhere. "I don't think the five horse'll stop today," one plunger said. "I think he'll keep running right to the finish." Every now and then the Racing Secretary's voice—he was responsible for writing the Condition Book and carding the races—came over the loudspeaker to make a plea. "Gentlemen," he might say, "your attention, please, we need help in the fourth on Tuesday, we're short two horses," and some trainer who owed him a favor or had a horse he wanted to run for exercise would go to the office and enter the nag to fill out the field. Management liked large fields, especially in exacta races, because they made for wacky odds and bank-breaking payoffs. "I had that exacta the other day," somebody said, "the nine-hundred-dollar one, only I didn't play it." The hay wagon roared by outside, collecting dirty straw, followed by the water wagon, dust control, whose driver seemed to like nothing better than dousing people. Everywhere last-minute connections were being made before the security guards chained shut the two backstretch phone booths, sealing off the community from bookies and would-be fixers until after the ninth race.

II

Gary Headley, the trainer, and his groom, Bo Twinn, were having coffee the first time I visited their barn. They sat in lawn chairs, smoking and reading the *Form,* and rested their cups on a round low-slung table made from a salvaged telephone-cable spool. There were doughnuts on the table, and empty almond packs and soda cans. Both men looked tired and dirty after the morning's work. Headley's blue nylon windbreaker was creased as though he'd slept in it, and his blond hair wandered off in random shocks. Bo hadn't shaved yet and his face looked old and raw. It was the sort of face that occurred in hot dusty places. I'd seen it before in Depression-era photographs. Over the years Bo had developed a crusty personality to match his face, and he could be formidably short-tempered on occasion, but he loved horses and they loved him. "If you was smart, you wouldn't have to ask that question," he would say, pursing his lips like a schoolmarm. Headley, who was in his late thirties and younger than Bo, took great pride in employing him. "Best groom on the grounds," he'd say confidentially, hiding his mouth behind a hand, "and the best paid, too." There was no way to substantiate such statements and besides, Headley made them all the time.

He was a hyperbolic and something of a flake, not the best trainer at Golden Gate but also not the worst. His life so far had been a model of fluctuant behavior. His brother Bruce, a respected trainer on the southern California circuit, had hired Gary out of high school, taught him the trade, and introduced him around, but Gary had never been able to commit himself absolutely to the track, not for any length of time. He'd work for a while, building up his business, then wash out and drift through odd jobs in the real world, or (if he had a little money saved) stay in his apartment behind closed curtains, sipping wine and watching TV. Then he'd decide that training horses really was right for him, and he would go back to work, starting at the bottom, and keep at it for a few years before becoming disillusioned or bored or upset and washing out again. Headley recognized the pattern but seemed incapable of breaking it. This was his major problem. The track, like any subculture, extracted a mean price for ambivalence, and Headley had been paying it too long. His marriage to a legal secretary, a woman who knew nothing about racing, had recently fallen apart, and the failure bothered him. "First divorce in the family in seven generations," he said, as though reminding himself. These days, almost in compensation, he seemed more dedicated than he had in the past, although the odds were even that he might flipflop momentarily, disappearing from the backstretch without leaving a forwarding address.

"It's a lot safer in here than it is outside," he said, stuttering as he did when he got excited. "Take a walk through downtown Oakland some time, you'll see what I mean. You'll probably get your throat slit. You ever see any of those movies about racing? They're not true. All the trainers wear striped suits. They have molls around and screw them in the stalls. Maybe that happened once, but it's not that way, not really. There's a few bad apples, but you can still leave your tack room unlocked, and when you come back your stuff's still there. It's much worse outside. If you don't believe me, go take a walk in Oakland, you'll get cut up so bad you'll look like spaghetti."

Bo had other problems. He lived in a tack room, a compact space, fifteen by twenty feet, ordinarily used for storing saddles, bridles, and the like, and two female cats had adopted his residence as their own and presented him with ten kittens. "I got all kinds of cats," he said, showing me the litter nursing on his bed. The room smelled overpoweringly feline. There was a TV set on the bureau, a few shirts hanging from a rod inside an open closet, and pictures of horses taped to the walls. "The two mama cats, they take turns nursing. I never did see anything like it before. One nurses and then the other. This kitten here's the prettiest," he said, picking up a long-haired calico by the scruff. "I might even keep her. Don't know what I'll do with them others, though. I got 'em in every possible color. That little guy over there, he's the runt. They push him around. Maybe you'd like a cat for your house?"

Headley took me around his barn, which he shared with Bud Keen, another trainer. Keen kept a goat in his section to help quiet a high-strung filly, and when the goat saw us coming he backed off, making goat noises. Headley had six stalls, and the horses in them were all hurting in one way or another. "Think this horse is sound?" he asked rhetorically, stopping in front of a bedraggled-looking mare. "She's raced twice in six months, that's how sound she is. I could get a better class of horse but I don't want the hassle. I used to train a big string at Santa Anita, but the owners drove me nuts. See this?" he asked, pointing to a deep cleft between his eyebrows. "I got this from worrying."

Next he showed me a handsome two-year-old, Urashima Taro, who hadn't raced yet. "I think this colt's a winner," he said. "This colt's my dream horse. I already nominated him for the Derby, the Belmont, and the Preakness. It's cheaper to pay the entry fees now than waiting." We continued down the shedrow. "See this filly? She was crazy when she came in. I couldn't even touch her. She was wrecked. Her owners are nice people, though. For a change. They gave me plenty of time with her. Now she's rounding into shape. What are those people, Bo? The Sandomirs. What are they? They speak Spanish, but I know they're not Mexicans. The wife speaks English pretty good. I think they might be Panamanian. Are those people Panamanian, Bo?"

"All's I know is they're not Mexicans," Bo said.

"No, they're not Mexicans. I think they might be Panamanians."

"What's the filly's name?" I asked.

"Pichi," Headley said. "Don't ask me what it means."

III

I never met Gregory Sandomir, a native of Argentina, but his wife, Mary, once explained his involvement in racing quite succinctly. "My husband has the feeling since he's very young," she told me. "He likes the horses very much." Sandomir, who manufactures Rolling-brand blue jeans in Los Angeles, had always wanted to own a thoroughbred, and in the summer of 1976 he began shopping around. He knew some trainers, and they sent him to various breeding farms and ranches to look at the stock for sale, but it took a while before he found what he wanted. At Sledge Stable and Walnut Wood Farm in Hemet, California, he fell for an eight-month-old chestnut filly by Dr. Marc R out of Atomic Jay. Sandomir knew little about conformation (the ideal physical structure of a thoroughbred) or bloodlines (its all-important heritage), but this served him well because the filly had nothing much to commend her except for a distant, minimal relationship to War Admiral, which might have accounted for her willful nature. She was pretty and excitable, and Sandomir, thoroughly smitten, made the purchase and named her Pichi. This had been his daughter's nickname and she was married now and gone from his house.

As a two-year-old, Pichi was consigned to a Hollywood Park trainer who had no tolerance for her vicissitudes, and soon she was locked into a battle of wills. She resisted most stringently at the starting gate. She hated the machinery and balked whenever she went near it. Instead of trying to ease her in, comforting her, the trainer apparently used force, which aggravated matters. Horses who have an aversion to the gate can usually be counted on to break poorly in a race, sometimes a half-second behind the field, and Pichi followed the rule. In her first race, a five-and-a-half-furlong sprint (eight furlongs equal a mile), she finished eighth by thirteen lengths, and two weeks later, against weaker opponents, she loped home tenth, twelve casual lengths behind the leader. Sandomir became concerned about her condition. She didn't look well. There was no reason, he thought, to extract victory from a horse's hide, so when the meet ended and the action shifted to Delmar, he arranged for Pichi to be trained by Ross Fenstermaker, who ran her twice at a mile. She improved, breaking better both times, but she was still far from winning a race or even finishing in the money. Fenstermaker would've stayed with her, but he got an offer to train a string of first-class horses for Fred Hooper, an owner of some prominence. Owners like Hooper tend to demand exclusivity from their trainers in exchange for the privilege of working with quality stock, so Fenstermaker had to get rid of his outlaw. His old friend Gary Headley was just getting back into the game at Golden Gate, and he urged Sandomir to give Headley a try. The competition was much cheaper in the north, and Pichi would have a better chance at breaking her maiden. Fenstermaker gave Headley a single caution: Watch this filly, Gary, she's murder in the gate.

Pichi arrived by van in February 1978, toward the end of a long cold wet winter that had broken the back of a two-year drought. Rivers were running again, the snowpack was deep around the Sierras, and Pichi, who'd spent a few months standing in mud, had an awful-looking pair of hind legs, raw and infected. Headley led her to his barn, Number Twenty-Five, a cobwebby structure located in nonpreferential territory among the shops of feed merchants, tack salesmen, and purveyors of riding silks, at least a quarter mile from the track. He examined his new charge and thought, *Shit, another cripple.* He had plenty of cripples on hand already, representing varying degrees of unsoundness, here a grapefruit-size knee, there a quarter-cracked hoof, and Pichi fit right in. She hadn't raced for half a year and was in miserable shape. Headley found a crescent-shaped scar on her rib cage and figured that somewhere along the line a groom must have hit her with something heavy and broken her rib. But the rib appeared to have mended on its own, although imperfectly. She had other imperfections as well. The tip of her tail was missing, nipped off in a starting gate accident, and when she ran, her uterus opened abnormally wide and she sucked air through it, which caused muscle spasms in her back. She also had what Headley called "psychological" problems. She was tense and feisty and wouldn't let anybody touch her. Nor would she eat, no matter what was served—oats, hay, some special mix— and she was mean-tempered and kicked at Bo whenever she could. When she wasn't acting up, she remained aloof, staring at the rear wall of her stall like an infanta trapped in a tower, her regal bearing violated, and she flicked her tail at passersby and pinned her ears at the slightest provocation.

Fortunately Headley liked working with cripples. They were puzzles to him, engines in need of tinkering, and it gratified him to watch a jockey boot home a horse who only a month before had been hobbled and sulky, totally unfit. He would've preferred working with good stakes horses, but such animals were not his current lot and he was realistic enough not to suffer from their absence. He liked Sandomir because Sandomir didn't push. Some owners demanded that their horse run every ten days regardless of condition, even if it meant injecting an unstable joint with cortisone, but Sandomir was willing to accumulate feed and veterinary bills, which could be staggering, until Pichi felt better. So Headley proceeded slowly. He began by having a vet sew up her uterus, mitigating the air-sucking problem, and gave her Robaxin, a muscle relaxant, for her back. Then he started her exercise program, walking first, then some light galloping. Bo worked on her legs, applying poultices, liniment, and bandages, talking to her in his cranky old flatlands voice. "She's a radical son-of-a-bitch," he would say, mixing genders freely, but he was pleased when at last he could clean her stall without expecting to catch a hoof in the middle of his forehead.

One morning when she seemed particularly calm, Headley decided to school her in the starting gate. He was a little apprehensive, recalling Fenstermaker's warning, but she seemed so placid and yielding he thought she might be ready. When Pichi got to the schooling area, back in the shade of some twisted live oaks, she went wild. She attacked the gate, kicking and rearing, and when it failed to collapse under her ministrations she tried to jump over it. This was precisely as feasible as a cow jumping over the moon. Her exercise rider, taking up on the reins, managed to restrain her and lead her away before she injured herself. Headley was incredulous but he kept schooling her patiently, with greater supervision, until she went into the machinery without resisting and stood there moderately still, waiting to be released.

IV

Pichi's aversion made me curious about starting gates, so I went to the schooling area—it was located near the Corporation Yard, where track equipment like harrows was stored—and talked to Bob Yerian, Golden Gate's starter, about them. Yerian was from

Montana and looked uncannily like Will Rogers. He told me the track leased two gates from the Puett company. Each weighed between thirteen and fourteen tons and had fourteen post positions. The rear doors of the pens were held closed by a latch-type affair. The front doors, the ones which snapped open abruptly at the start of a race, were spring-loaded and held together by electromagnets. When Yerian pressed his buzzer, the gate's two power cells (two others were always charged and ready, a backup system) shut down, springing the magnets, and the front doors were thrown open all at once. An eight-man crew supervised the loading procedure, which took, under optimal conditions, no more than five seconds per horse, or about a minute for a twelve-horse field.

Yerian would have gone on for quite some time, but he saw a worker over in the Corporation Yard trying to guide a water truck through a small space between his, Yerian's, car and a tree, and he went running off, which left me standing next to a member of the gate crew whom Yerian had been calling Slick. I couldn't see anything slick about him, but he was nice enough and full of interesting observations.

"Today's the only kind of day I really want a boat," said Slick, looking out at the sailboats on the Bay and the San Francisco skyline behind them. "Isn't it gorgeous out there? Look at that bridge. The city always looks different to me. Some days it's right up on top of you and other days it's way off in the distance."

This statement about the watery nature of apparently solid phenomena was pertinent to my situation. The Tanforan meeting was only five days old, but already I'd lost a third of my stake.

V

All gamblers look for signs, and I was given an appropriate one that first week when a filling from one of my molars popped out of its rightful place and into a wad of gum. My tongue, acting involuntarily, began immediate explorations of the hole. The image of *emptiness* should have been transported to my brain, but it was not and I kept losing steadily. Naturally I had alibis, and ample time in which to consider them, but in the end they had no effect on the ledger, which was negative, pal, negative. During one inglorious sixteen-race period I picked nine consecutive losers. Six of them finished out of the money entirely. Nobody else was doing so poorly, of that I was certain. Scrawny old guys in Panama hats and suspenders were cashing in at the fifty-dollar window and old ladies playing systems based on the sum of their nieces' birthdays divided by the pills in an Anacin bottle were hitting the daily double daily. They jumped, they howled, they clapped their hands and shed joyful tears, and I wanted to bust their kneecaps with a baseball bat.

Losers form strange partnerships; I formed mine with Arnold Walker. Together we licked our wounds. I thought Arnold resembled a diplomat in his elegant pin-striped suits and Caesar Romero locks, fog-gray and fragrant as pastilles. The Turf Club matrons loved him. He looked like an envoy sent from a far country for the express purpose of breaking hearts. If all gamblers share a common innocence, a nostalgic longing for a condition prior to habituation, then Arnold was a superior gambler by virtue of his superior innocence. He refused steadfastly to learn anything from experience, and even winning thousands of dollars did not satisfy him for long. What he wanted couldn't be found at the track, but there was no telling this to him. He'd spent a lifetime avoiding the truth. He was fifty-three, thrice-married, and his face, tanned to a Boca Raton brown even in April, was entirely absent of lines.

Arnold liked me because I was a writer. "Writers are class," he said. During the Second World War, he claimed to have seen

Hemingway in the lobby of the Waldorf-Astoria with a Gorgeous Broad on his arm and a glass of champagne in his hand, and he continued to believe that such events, bubbly and tit-ridden, occurred frequently in writers' lives. One night he insisted on buying me dinner and made me order lobster. Arnold had inherited a chain of drugstores on the Peninsula and wanted to show me that money meant nothing to him, but of course it did. Over drinks he confessed to being down three grand for the year. "Down at Del Mar once," he said, cracking a lobster claw, "I had the best day of my life. I hit two exactas big and won thirty-eight hundred dollars. Then I went to a party and picked up a movie star and laid her." He looked cautiously around before whispering her name. I didn't believe him for a second.

Beyer and his speed figures were the first thing I threw out of my handicapping support system, not because Beyer was wrong or inaccurate but because using figures went against my grain. I was learning that to win you had to work within the net of your own perceptions. For me speed had negative connotations. It was too American a preoccupation, too insistently the grammar of motorcyclists and technologists. *Passo a passo si va lontano,* I heard them say in Florence, step by step one goes a long way, and this accent on the qualitative aspects of a journey was more to my liking. So I decided to concentrate on factors like class and condition, relegating speed to a secondary position except when it appeared to be the single factor separating one horse from all the others.

But even after making this adjustment, I lost again the next afternoon. The track, it seemed, was just like life, unjust and aleatory. Muggers won handily, thieves tripled their bankrolls, and murderers walked whistling to the parking lot, their blades secured in fat green sheaths. I felt in tune with the grandstand ironist who saw two losers scuffling and shouted at them, "Cut it out, you guys, this is the sport of kings." Then Emery Winebrenner, trainer, backstretch bon vivant, and self-proclaimed handicapper *extraordinaire,* said, "You're losing? Come and sit with me in the owner-trainer section this afternoon and I'll get your money back for you," and again I had reason to believe.

VI

I met Winebrenner by accident. One morning I hooked up with Buck Ball, a horseshoer, and watched him work at several barns. He had a barrel chest and giant smithy arms and navigated the shedrows in an extremely lived-in camper. It took him about twenty minutes to replace old shoes with new ones. He stood in an uncomfortably stooped position while working and I was feeling sorry for him until I calculated that he probably earned twenty grand a year hammering nails into hoofs. This seemed another example of cosmic injustice. Buck stopped at Winebrenner's to shoe a fat sullen nag who'd just returned from a six-month vacation on the farm. A groom named Bob Ferris held the horse steady. He affected a tough-guy pose, dangling a cigarette from his lip and speaking in a curt monotone, but he turned out to be the most literate person I encountered on the backstretch. Most of his reading had been done during a sojourn in the slammer. Ferris had a taste for bad jokes and he told me one about an Englishman who kept an aviary for breeding rooks. When the Englishman's pals dropped by they always asked, "Bred any good rooks lately?" Ferris thought the joke was a real killer and he laughed and stomped out his cigarette. "Know what it takes to be a groom?" he asked. "Only two things: you have to know how to shovel shit and how to say *whoa!*" His eyes were watering a little. He really loved this stuff. Another man emerged from a nearby stall, blinking into the light. He was stocky and thick-chested like Buck, with a soft round face, a little mustache, and dark hair beginning to thin conspicuously at the crown. His eyes were brown, glazed, and abstracted. Because he'd been separating straw from manure I took him to be a groom, too, but this was Winebrenner himself. He had difficulty speaking.

"I can't talk today," he said when I asked him about a horse of his I'd seen working out that morning. "Today's a bad day. Maybe you could come by tomorrow. Tomorrow's much better." We shook hands and he wandered off and lifted the hood of his pickup and began tinkering distractedly with the spark plugs.

Later I learned that such silences were not uncommon with Emery. He sometimes got deeply involved in interior processes and couldn't easily extricate himself. I came to imagine entire worlds within his body, miniature crystalline structures of surpassing intricacy. When he wasn't lost in silence he was out there hustling. He loved to hustle and the backstretch was his life. He rented a quiet house in San Pablo surrounded by oak trees, but he seldom went there except to shower and change clothes. Instead he preferred to wander the shedrows or work at his barn, even pitchforking manure, or go to the races. The house served him as a psychic safety zone and he was proud of it and the library he kept there. Often he reminded me that he owned every available book on training methods. "If you ever need a book," he said, "just ask me. If I don't have it, I'll buy it and you can borrow it from me."

Emery was alarmingly generous, a manic spender who doled out free passes, hot tips, and spare change to almost anybody who asked. In the cafeteria once I tried to pay for my coffee and his soft drink and he countered by picking up the tab for everybody else in line, including a groom who was already well into the Old Milwaukees and listing badly to the left. Old Milwaukee could do this to you. It was a Schlitz second brand sold in the track cafeteria, and whenever I saw the Old Milwaukee slogan, "Tastes as great as its name," I wanted to make a house arrest of the advertising geniuses who'd been paid a million dollars to think it up. Anyway, the groom was listing, and he lifted his can in salute. "Cheers, Emry," he said. Nobody ever pronounced that middle "e." The vowel was elided and *Emery* was given the same high-pitched nasal treatment *filly* got.

In 1977 Winebrenner had had a fair year for a young trainer. He'd started his horses a hundred and twenty-three times, won seventeen races, and been in the money exactly one-third of the time. He'd earned a total of $74,347 in purses. But this year he'd been slow to start because a few of his old standbys, like Little Coop's and Equivalent Model, were used up and not really producing any more. Soon he'd have to start dropping them in class, hoping they'd be "claimed," or bought, by other trainers before their problems were more graphically revealed. At the same time he was scouting replacements. He had twelve head now and wanted more. Every day he read the *Form* and searched for horses who were being badly handled and cut short of their potential. Such errors showed up in the statistics. Golden Gate supported a small colony of incompetent trainers who survived by charm or guile or pure hucksterism, and sometimes they made such blatant mistakes that it was a simple matter to claim good stock away from them. They ran sprinters in routes and routers in sprints, sent horses to post without first teaching them how to change leads on the turns, let faders go right on fading without once trying to build their stamina, scrimped on feed and tack, and hired help whose talents were better suited to street fighting than caring for thoroughbreds. "You're seeing me in a low phase," Emery said on days when the dark depressive clouds were massed in his skull. "Last year I was really hot. It'll be that way again after I make some claims. I bet I'll be in good shape at Bay Meadows this fall. It just takes time."

I enjoyed visiting Emery's barn. A radio hung from a hook near a stall and played rock and good jazz all morning long, and Ferris talked about books and racing and his Exactamobile, an old Chevy purchased with the proceeds from a thousand-dollar exacta. Most grooms had no transportation at all, so the Exactamobile was a heady sign of independence. With it Ferris could go anywhere, whenever he wanted, even back to his hometown, Port Townsend, Washington. The barn seemed to attract a younger crowd, people looking for work, people looking for information, people with scams and illogical systems, other trainers, jockeys, and even groupies, and Emery welcomed them all unless it was a bad day, in which case the barn doors were shut and the radio was turned off. Though he often traveled through the grandstand with an entourage, Emery felt his glad-handing image was at odds with his essential self, which was finer and more percipient. "I have lots of acquaintances," he told me once, making what for him was an important distinction, "but very few friends. The acquaintances are good acquaintances but they're not close to me. I've always been a loner." Someday, he said, he wanted to live on a ranch in rugged isolated terrain, maybe in the mountains. He wanted to have a big garden and grow vegetables and raise cattle and stable a few horses. He didn't know exactly how the ranch would come to pass but the vision, as he presented it, was a felt thing, immediately palpable, and when he spoke of it I could see its dimensions, the split-pine fence and rustic ranch house, and around it snowcapped peaks of granite.

VII

On the appointed day, the day I was going to get my money back, I didn't have to stop by Winebrenner's barn. I ran into him just after dawn. He was standing at the rail among other trainers, dressed in jeans and a western shirt, spitting snuff-tinged saliva into the dust, and watching Cohasset Prince, a nice two-year-old of his, work three furlongs. He seemed glad to see me. Overnight his spirits had regenerated and he was barely able to stand still.

"You want to talk, eh?" he asked, hitching up his jeans. "Well, you picked the right guy. I love to talk. What do you want to talk about? Racing? I've always been into racing. First thing I raced was pigeons. That's right, pigeons. I grew up in southern California, near L.A. My mother was Mexican and my father was half-Mexican and half-German. That's where the Winebrenner comes from, the German. My parents were divorced when I was about one. My grandmother raised me. She was a typical Mexican grandmother. A lot of people don't know I'm part Mexican. They don't think I look it." He paused to spit and watch a young blond girl walk by. She looked familiar, and then I remembered I'd seen her dancing at the Home Stretch. "Track's much better than it used to be," Emery said. "More young people around. Not so many derelicts, know what I mean?

"I started with the pigeons when I was thirteen or fourteen. Every so often the different clubs get together and have a race. The start is really incredible. The starters take all the birds to a central place, then throw them in the air, all at once, hundreds of them, and they fly off in flocks at first but pretty soon they get their bearings and start to home. I found a pigeon out here one day, by the barns, he still had a band on his leg. His wing was broken. I fixed it up with splints and let it heal and then I let him go. I guess he finished *that* race a little late." Emery chuckled, rubbing his mustache. "You know what I raced after pigeons. *Dragsters.* You remember Don Garlits? Big Daddy Roth? When I quit with cars I took up with horses. You see how it worked? It was a logical progression."

That afternoon I joined him in the section of the grandstand reserved for owners and trainers. He was sitting with his friend Richard Labarr, a bearded black-haired former beautician in his middle thirties. Labarr was a classic case of somebody who'd given up a comfortable life in the freeway universe to become a racetrack gypsy. While running his beauty shop in Sacramento, he met a trainer who got him interested in racing, and then, on a whim, to impress a girl friend, he bought a horse for twenty-five hundred bucks. Horses don't come much cheaper and at first Labarr wasn't sure what to do with his bargain-basement purchase. After a couple of false starts he connected with Emery, and Emery got the horse into shape and the horse went on to break his maiden at the Vallejo fair, paying forty dollars to win. Labarr had bet fifty dollars across the board. I asked him how it felt. "Like an orgasm," he said, "the best orgasm you ever had." The horse won almost twenty grand in purses before Labarr had to get rid of him. Then he got rid of the beauty shop. Now he was hanging around Golden Gate and trying to make it as a jockeys' agent. He represented two apprentices, Dennis Rond and a cocky kid named Jay Jsames, but neither of them was live and Labarr wasn't getting them many mounts. So instead, to make ends meet, he played exactas, drew on his savings, and gave an occasional on-site haircut to trainers too busy to go to a barbershop.

"I like the five-six, six-five," Labarr said. "And maybe toss in the eight. What do you think, Em'ry?"

"I like the one horse. You can't leave out the three horses, either."

Emery told me that he played only exactas, the rest of the action was chickenfeed. He liked the figuring, the various possible angles, the maximal returns. For two races I sat still, waiting in suspense for pearly wisdom to drop from his lips, but he was losing himself and seemed to have forgotten his promise to get me even. When the horses went to post for the next race I left him to place a bet, and when the horse I played, Poppy's Rose, won by a nose I was supremely excited.

"Hey," Emery said, "I thought you were losing." He was amused that I'd showed so much emotion, violating the code of racetrack cool. Pros were supposed to accept even thousand-dollar payoffs without batting an eye. "Maybe you can help me," he said, kidding.

Already Labarr was looking ahead to the seventh race.

"Let's baseball one-five-seven," he said, suggesting they buy tickets on all the possible combinations.

"Can't," Emery said, "five's been scratched."

I asked him if trainers could remove a horse from a race even if the horse wasn't hurting, and he said yes, scratches were used as tactical maneuvers. If another entry clearly outclassed yours, it made sense to withdraw and wait for a better day. The stewards didn't care, he said, unless you scratched your horse from a short field, one with only five or six entries. Scratches were often legitimate, though.

"I scratched a horse once because he just looked bad. An old groom told me he wouldn't last the night and then the vet came and told me the same thing. The horse was hemorrhaging internally. I was with him when he died. All of a sudden he started kicking. I had to dive out of the stall head first. He started bucking around, bouncing off the walls, just like a big fish flopping on a boat deck. It lasted about thirty seconds and then he shivered and died. You go through strange things with horses. One time I had a colicky horse and he got so congested we had to hold him up and walk him back and forth along the shedrows just like you'd walk a junky."

By the ninth race we were both down and I gave up any hope of winning. When we left the grandstand the wind was blowing hard off the Bay, very cold for April, and blown-about programs took brief flight with the gulls before sinking into the whitecaps.

"I never get cold," Emery said with a laugh as I pulled on a sweater. "I don't know why. People are always kidding me about it. They don't understand it at all."

We stopped at the backstretch cafeteria for something to drink, and a small man, uninvited, sat down at our table. His hair was wet and freshly combed and he wore round scholarly glasses and chewed nervously on his lip. He looked as if he'd taken four thousand night school classes, the eternal student. Emery seemed to know him but it was a while before I recognized Bob Ferris behind those lenses. He'd slipped into a new identity, something different for a Home Stretch Saturday night. The transformation was shocking. It reminded me of Emery's house in the hills.

"Once I lived in a tack room," Emery said. "This was before I got my trainer's license. I had that room all fixed up. I had a color TV, a hot plate with two burners, a tape deck. I even had a coffee can to piss in so I wouldn't have to stumble around in the middle of the night." I could see that he was winding down now, collapsing toward those crystalline structures. "I don't really mind living alone. I go places in my head. I love my work, you know, but I don't know if I'll ever really be happy. It's weird, isn't it? I mean, I just don't know."

I listened for a bit longer, stirring my coffee, until I was convinced nothing would be resolved by hanging around. Later I wondered why I had spent so much time with Emery, what I'd expected to learn from him. The answer was clear, though. We were both struggling; his confusion resembled my own.

VIII

On Sunday I went exploring. People were out there after Nature, crowding into Tilden Park above Albany and spreading their blankets under the trees and cracking open one beer after another because the weekend was almost over and the dismal part of the cycle was about to begin again. The carousel was still in operation and children were clamoring for rides. They climbed into the saddles or were held in place by attentive parents, and they went round and round to the music, which was the same fulminating Sousa-type stuff that had been playing for the last half-century. The horses were splendid, though, with braided manes and tensed legs and heads thrown back. They appeared to be smiling, but that was the woodcarver's improvisation, a touch of anthropomorphic color for the masses.

At San Pablo Reservoir I saw a boy at the fish-cleaning table gutting a huge black bass. He'd caught it earlier on a Jitterbug. There weren't many bass in the reservoir and he'd been lucky to get one. He showed me where he'd caught it, back in some reeds.

"Here's the exact spot," he said. "I'm going to try again tonight."

"Give me a number," I said, thinking his luck might rub off on me.

"A number?"

"Any number. First one that pops into your head."

"Four," he said. "Is that right?"

In the valley below there was a stable offering pony rides and again the children went round, this time circling a fenced oval strewn with manure. They rode more cautiously than they had on the carousel, holding tightly to the reins, and each backward glance they took seemed a daring enterprise. Kodaks clicked. The ponies looked worn and tired, and green flies as big as thumbnails trailed them wherever they went.

All the shopping malls were busy, and in them a different music obtained, thin and reedy. It had the consistency of aural linoleum and played at varying tempi because the tapes were old and hopelessly fouled and sometimes skittered from "Raindrops Keep Falling on My Head" to "Tie a Yellow Ribbon 'Round the Old Oak Tree" without any segue. Nobody cared; they were busy consuming electric hot-dog cookers and cases of STP and room deodorizers that smelled like the aspens being felled in the Sierras to make way for ski condominiums.

At dusk I drove through Oakland. The first hookers were out and they wore wigs and hotpants and had long legs and impressive bodies. Johns cruised the avenue, maybe the same husbands who'd been shopping earlier, and in separate cars their teen-aged sons, drunk on two beers and dribbling down their shirts, too frightened of the ladies and their legs to do anything but insult them. They pressed beery faces to the windows, and as desire receded into their bones they got a little crazier, a little more mean. In the future they'd build empires, but for now the cops would protect them from error, arresting the hookers instead and turning the experience into something slick and voyeuristic as a centerfold. "I like to see movies, then read the books they are made from," said Vicki Witt, the Playmate-of-the-Month, enunciating the American dilemma, the valuation of illusion over substance, what can be touched.

IX

And then it was night. When did the switchback occur, I wondered, lying alone in bed remembering spring nights long ago and the warm hazy unforeboding darkness of neighboring territories. Playing stickball under a streetlight, chasing a bright pink rubber ball beyond the arc of the visible, searching for it in pitch-black yards with the smell of grass in the air and no threats studding the dark, the night infrangible, serene. No races to go to, the racing all inside. When did the switchback occur? Not in Florence when I walked the streets after midnight with pockets full of *lire,* funny money, and not later in Africa when I stumbled home from Edwin's shop with its shelves of tinned corned beef and viscous condensed milk, stumbling blindly into the bush of snakes and keening sounds, brain stunned by Star beer or palm wine or native weed. What was I *doing* there? What was I doing *here?* When did the switchback occur? Headley was right, all sorts of things were waiting for you just outside, many serious possibilities, guns, sharks, muggers, tumors. Renaissance Florentines were preoccupied with death, with its repetitions and flourishes, and devised improbable theories to account for same. Even the French were "concerned." Bodin, *Method for the Easy Understanding of Histories,* 1556, turned to numerology, danger zones on the biological grid. "No one considering this matter attentively doubts that the death of men occurs in multiples of seven and nine: as 14, 18, 21, 27, 28, 35, 36, 42, 45, 49, 56. But if the seventh concurs with the ninth all antiquity agreed that it was a most perilous year." Sixty-three, the climacteric, Aristotle, Boccaccio, Erasmus, Luther. Six and three, seven and nine, exacta probables, inescapable failings. What I was waiting for now was not sleep but the next switchback, acceptance.

Chapter Four

I came to think of trainers as Renaissance princes who ruled the backstretch. Walking the shedrows I saw that each barn resembled a principality, embodying a unique blend of laws and mores, an individuated style. Brightly colored placards bearing trainers' names or initials or devices shone in the sun, and it was possible to intuit the flesh of a prince from the sign he displayed. If Eldon Hall's escutcheon showed a white dollar sign on a green background, then it stood to reason that Hall would be tall and lean and southern, wearing an expensive Stetson and specializing in speedy Kentucky-bred two-year-olds. Jake Battles's colors of red and optic blue suggested a feisty raw-faced character who rode his pony belligerently and wore a monumental turquoise ring on the finger of one hand. Emery Winebrenner's placard was simple, the letters EW rendered in sunny yellow against a field as black and sunken as night.

Inside the barns I always noticed the music first, rock, soul, or jazz if the help was young, MOR if older, and mariachi or salsa if Spanish-speaking. Grooms sometimes had a fiesta going on, with liquid refreshments and the smell of burning hemp in evidence, but more often a barn's atmosphere was determined by the trainer and reflected his personality. At the Stewarts', where the whole family worked together, the area around the stalls was neat and clean and felt like a suburban living room. There were no beer cans blocking paths, no syringes left lying in the dust. Tom Stewart was neat and clean and soft-spoken, and so was Bonnie Stewart, mother and assistant trainer, and so were the Stewart children, who helped out after school and on vacations. As a hobby, the family raised lop-eared rabbits, and three rotund specimens, Samantha, Tabitha, and Pumpkin, gazed out at the passing world from a mesh cage by the stalls. Plumpness was a primary characteristic of the breed, something to be encouraged, and these bunnies had it in abundance. They looked to me like mutant creatures, victims of radiation or BHT.

Some trainers filled their barns with female assistants, courtly ladies-in-waiting. Winebrenner always had at least one looker working for him, and Eric Longden and Craig Roberts could usually be counted on for one or two. Women, it was rumored, as though their presence needed excusing, had wonderful hands, healing hands, and a gentle way with nervous fillies, but this sort of myth always prevailed in masculine enclaves. A few women trainers worked at Golden Gate, including aces like Kathy Walsh, but they weren't yet a challenge to the old guard, and the backstretch remained for the moment the dominion of princes. Bill Mastrangelo carried himself erect as a soldier, with a slight swagger to his step, and ran his crew with military efficiency. Chuck Jenda, an ex-radical from Berkeley who used to pledge ten percent of his Santa Anita handicapping earnings to the Cause, favored the style of a taciturn football coach. He wore a Michigan Wolverines' cap and spoke of his grooms as his "team." "Was I bluffing or not?" asked Jenda, after dropping down a sound horse to steal a claiming race. "Only the people on our team knew for sure!" Jenda had gotten his start walking hots and working as a groom, and so had most other trainers, including Headley and Winebrenner. Bobby Martin, perennially the top trainer at Golden Gate, had said goodbye to Kansas when he was seventeen, jumped into a souped-up Mercury with foam dice above the dashboard, and driven nonstop to Chicago. But Chicago was cold even in the fall, and Martin, who'd had enough frigidity on the plains, packed up and headed for California, Land of Warmth and Opportunity, where he landed a job breaking yearlings. Next he was galloping horses and then training them. Mastrangelo was a former jockey whose father had taken him to tracks and hustled him rides. Bobby Jennings had been a jockey, too, a six-footer who'd had to starve himself in order to make weight. Jennings's agent had been Bob Hack, whose uncle, Claude Turk, another jockey, had gotten Hack *his* first summer job as a groom. . . .

In fact the backstretch was as intricately nepotistic as the Medicis' Florence. Eric Longden, Johnny's son, trained a string of horses for his mother, while his father trained at Hollywood Park and Santa Anita, sometimes for his wife. Cliff de Lima trained for his wife, too, or so it said in the *Form,* and so did Ross Brinson, whose boy Clay—another son had been a jockey— worked down south among the Longden, Whittingham, and Barrera clans. Allen Auten, a handy apprentice, often rode for his father, Vern, and so many varied offspring worked for parents and uncles and aunts and grandfathers and grandmothers as part-time grooms they couldn't be counted. I kept expecting the Jukes to roll into town any minute, pulling horse vans behind their ratty pickup trucks.

Princes were busiest in the morning. Some of them liked to be right out there on the track, side by side with their stock, watching their horses exercise. Bobby Martin always commuted back and forth from the barn on his pony, along with his assistant, Les Silveria, who wore chaps and looked like a range rider. Bike Hixon, in snap-brim hat and cardigan, surveyed his charges from a saddle while devouring a big cigar. Walt Greenman often ponied his own animals, holding them by the reins while he galloped next to them, his thatch of prematurely white hair flying. This was the West, after all, or its last coastal echo, and these cowboy trainers were instinctual men. They distrusted language. Horses didn't talk anyway, or rather they spoke in gestures and signals which were best interpreted by touch. Sometimes a brief ride told you more about a horse's condition than hours of observation.

Other trainers, less physical types, congregated at the rail near Slaughterhouse Red. These princes had a taste for intrigue, for whispered conversations, for *secrets*. Among them quiet deals went down. Art Hirsch, duded up in Anaheim Moderne, jeans rolled into six-inch cuffs and silver hair arranged into an astoundingly mimetic duck's ass, beckoned to jockeys or agents, saying "Come on over here, let's talk for a minute, let's do a little business." Somebody else sidled up to Slaughterhouse and asked how fast Tornado, that mare of Trainer Y's, had worked, and Slaughterhouse put in a call to the clocker, whose job it was to record the workout times. "How the hell should I know?" the clocker complained, his disembodied voice floating out of a dented speaker near Slaughterhouse's ear. "There's so damn many of them out there!"

Trainers sometimes had difficulty keeping their principalities intact. Grooms got drunk and vanished, bouts of flu made the rounds and always lingered too long, deadly illnesses like founder shot forth from the clouds to skewer stakes-level performers, and crazy owner-kings were always demanding tribute, a table at the Turf Club or lobsters at Spenger's. Good stock was scarce at Golden Gate and it went mostly to the Martins and Mastrangelos, while lesser lights scrambled to make ends meet. Cheap horses were a nuisance. They went easily off form, stopped running the first time they met any opposition, and usually had no heart. The legend of Hirsch Jacobs and his horse Stymie, bought for fifteen hundred and returning almost a million, wasn't really any consolation. A patient trainer might squeeze one win per season from each baling-wire beauty, but the purses offered in low-level events were small indeed and barely covered costs. Pichi, when she deigned to eat, cost as much to feed as Alydar. Trainers charged owners about twenty dollars a day, plus veterinary bills, to stable a horse, but even the stingiest among them had trouble extracting a living wage from drips and drabs of double sawbucks.

Temptation, then, was everywhere, in every shedrow, and certain darkling princes were known to succumb on occasion. By sending a fit horse to post at high odds they could recoup at the pari-mutuel windows what they'd lost in feed. There were several time-honored tactics for influencing the outcome of a race. Superior workouts, for example, might not be listed in the *Form;* clockers made mistakes, especially at dawn. Horses could be worked until razor sharp at private training tracks, and trainers were under no obligation to make this information public. Sometimes unwary bugboys were given misleading prerace instructions and told to keep a rail-shy horse on the rail. Sometimes a trainer rode a bad jockey for a race or two, then switched to a pro. Sometimes a jockey was told that it might be beneficial to make slight errors in judgment coming into the stretch, to hold the mount in check too long or use him up too soon or go to the whip too late or not go to it at all. They made such mistakes genuinely and it was almost impossible to separate true from false. There were hundreds of ways to make a horse's past performance chart read like a clinical account of lameness, and it was surprising, given the ease with which the muddying could be effected, that most trainers chose to operate honestly.

Masking a horse's true condition was not considered a capital offense, but sudden form reversals, those miraculous wake-up victories that resulted in big payoffs, were punishable by law. They occurred nonetheless. Jockeys slapped batteries equipped with wire prongs—the device, held in the palm, was called a joint—to their mount's rump at the proper instant and held on as best they could while the poor electrified beast romped home. New drugs were constantly being developed, drugs for which no equine testing procedures had yet been devised—undetectable drugs—and these were administered in dark stall corners and soon thereafter sixty-to-one shots zoomed out of the gate like angels hyped on amphetamines. Those nags ran. They ran once and once only before slipping back into nagdom forever, but a hundred bucks selectively invested repaid six thousand big ones at any cashier's window on the grounds. These victories stood out, clearly evident, but stewards were slow to investigate. The unwritten rule around racetracks, not only at Golden Gate, seemed to be that you could get away with anything once, but repetition would cost you dearly. The penalties for such offenses were supposed to act as deterrents. Princes could be fined or suspended or banished from California, stripped of their license and sent packing to distant provinces where the summer county fair meet was the nonpareil of thoroughbred racing. Still, there were always a few backstretch blackguards who were willing to take the risk. Of them it could be written, as Burckhardt once wrote of the notorious Ludovico il Moro, that "no one probably would have been more astonished to learn that for the choice of means as well as ends a human being is morally responsible."

Most trainers, though, worked hard and chose to be scrupulous. They'd never have the chance to win a Triple Crown, but their honesty might someday be rewarded with the trainers' championship of Golden Gate Fields. "In so artificial a world," wrote Burckhardt, "only a man of consummate address could hope to succeed; each candidate for distinction was forced to make good his claims by personal merit and show himself worthy of the crown he sought."

II

I met Bobby Martin at his office, a musty tack room furnished with dilapidated armchairs and a vinyl-covered couch that belonged in a bus station. The office felt like Kansas, some inner sanctum on the plains with gas pumps out front and day-old newspapers for sale at the cash register. Martin sat behind a wooden desk and studied a large cardboard chart that listed all thirty-four of his horses and indicated by symbol whether they were scheduled to work (run hard over a specific distance, six furlongs, a mile, usually in preparation for a race), gallop, walk, or rest that morning. I had the impression that the chart wasn't really necessary, that Martin had long since memorized the data but wanted to give it an outward form and make it official. The chart was businesslike, professional, and so was the black phone on the desk, one of the few private lines I ever saw on the backstretch. These accoutrements suited Martin. He was a quietly confident man. He wore a rust-colored ski jacket and blue jeans with a dry cleaner's crease in them. His blondish hair was combed and he didn't look beaten down the way many trainers do when they hit forty.

Mike Haversack, a bugboy, sat opposite Martin and stirred the dust with his whip. He had the right face for pumping gas, thin, pale, with that curious racetrack hardness creeping in around the mouth. He galloped horses for Martin and sometimes got to ride a maiden. He lived in Pleasanton, as did the boss, and this seemed to work in his favor. "Hell," Martin said, "must be half the track lives out there." A groom led a big chestnut to the office door and Haversack stepped out of the office and into the stirrups. The transfer had a surreal quality, especially so early in the morning, but then again horses were always showing up in odd places. They filled the available space quite suddenly and I sometimes had the feeling of being pushed out of frame, like an actor snipped from a key scene. Another rider replaced Haversack on the couch, waiting in turn for his mount, and was soon replaced by yet another rider. The men were all dressed just like Martin, in ski jackets and jeans.

Ivan Puhich, Bill Mahorney's agent, stopped in to check on affairs. He was a big overwrought man, also wearing a ski jacket, who took himself and his job very seriously. One morning I'd tried to talk to him while he made his rounds, but he kept walking faster and faster, increasing the length of his stride—he stands six feet six—until I could no longer keep up with him. "If you can't keep up, we can't talk," Puhich said. "There's Bob Hack. Go talk to him, he walks slower." Martin also seemed to find Ivan a trifle overbearing, but he listened politely as Puhich told a convoluted story extolling his own virtues as an agent. He was representing Haversack and claimed to have saved the bugboy from a nefarious trainer's clutches. Apparently this trainer had asked Haversack to exercise one of his horses but hadn't stipulated a price to be paid for the job. "That bastard," Ivan said, "he tries to screw everybody. I told Mike, 'Don't you get on a horse unless I say so.' So the trainer says to him, 'You want a ride, Mike?' Mike says, 'I don't know. Talk to my agent.' So the trainer, he turns to me and says, 'Is it okay, Ivan?' 'Sure,' I tell him. 'Get on the horse, Mike.'" Ivan reached out a long arm and patted Haversack, who'd just returned, on the shoulder. "Mike, I want to commend you. You did the right thing." Poor Haversack, his cheeks red, sank embarrassedly into his boots. Martin slipped past Puhich, who was blocking the office door, and watched a filly on the hotwalker. She wasn't moving well. Her gait seemed awkwardly constricted. Martin stood watching her for a long time, his arms crossed over his chest.

Martin bought his first horse, Domingo Kid, when he was nineteen. He paid only seven hundred and fifty dollars because the horse, who'd once run in allowance races, was so brokedown and rank that nobody else wanted to deal with him. But Martin was young and ambitious and gradually conditioned the Kid and won eleven races with him that first year and twenty-six overall before he lost him to another trainer. Martin's name first appeared in the standings at Golden Gate in 1966, when he saddled ten winners in forty-three tries, and he has dominated them ever since. In 1978 he was pursuing his fifth consecutive championship and held a slim lead over Bill Mastrangelo, with whom he'd dueled before, most notably in 1975, when he'd won the title by only two victories. Though he tried to act nonchalant, Martin's eyes fired up whenever the championship was mentioned.

"It's not like golf or tennis," he said, "where you just go out and take somebody on head to head. Horses'll only do so much for you. You can't control 'em. Lot of people around here'd like to see me get beat. That's how it is when you're on the top."

Martin was exaggerating. No doubt a few malcontents wanted to see him collapse, but most people revered him. Young trainers wanted to be like him when they grew up, and old grooms said Bobby hadn't changed since he was a kid. He was honest and polite and never bullshitted you, or only a little. He treated his horses well and his grooms even better, paying them top dollar and refusing to inflict the usual psychic punishments. Even Tumwater Tom, who started early on his daily quota of Olympia and knew more about horses than most trainers, had stuck with Bobby. There was something of the classic Western hero in Martin's demeanor, the shy commanding presence of an Alan Ladd. He represented that most estimable racetrack quality, *class,* but his soft jawline and slightly lumpy nose would've kept him from ever playing opposite Maureen O'Hara.

There were two main reasons, beyond intelligence and hard work, for Martin's success: his expertise as a conditioner and his mastery of the claiming game. Conditioning a horse properly, getting him into shape and then keeping him fit, on form, was a craft little practiced at cheaper racetracks. Because of financial exigencies and near-terminal shortsightedness—some called it stupidity—trainers often pushed their horses much too hard in morning workouts, cranking them up for a single race, the clichéd Big Effort, and then afterward, when the horses returned to the barn feeling tired and sore, had to rest them for a month or two before running them again. This tactic made no sense but trainers pursued it zestfully, with oblivious devotion. The real key to conditioning was conservation. Energy expended in a race or workout had to be restored. So Martin kept close tabs on all his horses, checking their energy levels as he might the water in batteries, and designed for each of them an exercise program—the chart—that took into account individual strengths and weaknesses. He took the time to *know* his stock and so he got an optimal performance every race instead of one stellar showing followed by months of eights and nines.

Claiming was a more intricate and cerebral activity—it was known as the poker of the backstretch—but again success was dependent on knowing your stock. Any horse entered in such a race could be claimed, or purchased, for a predetermined price set by the Racing Secretary in the Condition Book. The idea was to create fields of roughly equivalent talent and value. In theory, trainers wouldn't enter a horse worth twenty grand in a race where the horse could be claimed by a rival for sixty-five hundred. But of course this happened all the time, because trainers, like their constituency, were gamblers. They were *always* looking for an edge.

Take, for instance, the hypothetical trainer Profit and his horse Lament, a four-year-old gelding who in the past month has finished fourth and second in two twelve-thousand-five-hundred-dollar claiming races. After such good performances, Profit might be expected to enter Lament at a higher level, say fourteen thousand, to protect him (Lament is clearly worth twelve-five), but Profit, a sharper, *drops* the horse in class and enters him in a race for a price tag of eighty-five hundred. This means one of three things: Lament is in bad shape, and Profit wants to get rid of him at a slight loss before Lament's true condition is known; Lament is *not* in bad shape but Profit wants others to think he is and thereby win a race against inferior opponents; Lament is just *beginning* to be in bad shape, getting old, with a kink in his step, and Profit is trying to make him look attractive, a bargain, while in fact he *wants* the horse to be claimed, having figured that the winner's share of the purse—four thousand—plus the claiming price—eighty-five hundred—will more than compensate him for the loss. The third tactic is the most difficult to master, predicated as it is on keen judgment, and Martin makes better use of it than anybody else at Golden Gate. Of the twenty-three head he'd "lost" since January, only three were worth feeding. Sometimes he got stung, this was inevitable, but more often than not his experiences echoed the early one with Domingo Kid. "I do a lot of speculating," Martin said. "You can't get too attached to the horses."

Martin was the only Golden Gate–based trainer whose horses

did well consistently on the tougher southern circuit. Every now and then he liked to assemble a caravan, sneak down to Hollywood Park, steal a few purses, then slip out of town. He smiled when he talked about these raids on Tinsel Town. I wondered why he didn't just set up shop in Los Angeles, or at least run a string there, but he said he made just as much money up north. This didn't compute. In 1977 Martin's horses won seventy-two races and a total of $456,287 in purse money, not much at all by southern standards. Actually, Martin hated L.A. "You ever been down there?" he asked. "It's like a jungle around those tracks." Bobby was still a good old boy at heart. On warm evenings he could still go out to his ranch in Pleasanton and do a little roping and riding and general whooping it up without having to worry that some criminal bastard was waiting just around the corner to steal his pinky ring, the one inset with his initials, RM, in diamonds.

The filly on the hotwalker was still having trouble. Martin went over and walked along next to her as she circled, and as he walked he touched her gently on the withers and said something inaudible. She seemed gradually to quiet, to understand her position in regard to the machine, and soon she was moving more fluidly, shaking her head and rippling her mane in the sun. Martin stayed with her for thirty minutes, linked to her movements, watching. The scene had a special air of transference. When Martin was satisfied with the filly's progress, he touched her a last time and went away.

III

I was about to leave the barn when Olivia Hernandez arrived to check on her baby. She worked for Martin and so did her husband, George, rubbing horses. For years she'd been trying to get pregnant without success, and then last fall, when she'd given up hope, she had missed a period. At first she refused to believe the implication, but the tests were all positive and she was still radiant now, two months after giving birth.

"You want to see her?" she asked. "Come in here, I'll show her to you."

We went into Martin's vacant office and Olivia knelt by the wall and removed a metal grate from the gas heater. When I knelt next to her and looked through the mesh, I could see into the tack room on the other side of the wall, where a dark-haired baby girl lay wrapped in bright pink blankets on an iron-frame cot.

"I could take you in there," Olivia said, "but I don't want to wake her. She's sleeping so soundly."

Her eyes were closed. She was surrounded by empty beer cans, bottles of liniment, unclipped rolls of Ace bandages trailing to the floor. Horses moved past the room, looking larger than ever in the low-ceilinged barn, going along the shedrow to their stalls. Olivia replaced the grate and we stood outside for a while, near the mounds of hay and sparrows bathing in puddles. Rogelio Gomez, the jockey whose broad cheekbones and deep-set eyes gave him the look of an Inca, rode by on an onyx-colored mare. He'd given the baby a stroller, but she was still too small to use it.

"*Como esta la niña?*" Gomez asked from his saddle.

"*Muy buena, Rogelio,*" Olivia said. Then she smiled, exhilarated, and said to me, "She's my miracle baby, you know."

IV

One morning I found a carved wooden owl hanging by a cord at the north end of the grandstand. The owl had been put there to keep starlings from nesting in the rafters, but above me I could see the birds flying in with bits of stolen hay in their beaks. This made me think of what I'd been reading about later Renaissance artists and the notions of dominance that had crept into their work. "Art is more powerful than nature," Titian had said. Giorgio Vasari, equally proud, had articulated a sentiment that Henry Ford might have approved. "Art today has been carried to such perfection," he said, "that, whereas our predecessors produced a picture in six years, we produce six in one year." Perfection as an aspect of *technique;* the power of nature *arrested.* Meanwhile the starlings went about their procreative business, peppering the bleachers with their droppings.

V

Glen Nolan had made his money operating a drayage company, but recently he'd diversified into a less predictable enterprise (a hobby for him, really) and now owned Nolan Farms, Inc., a ranch in Pleasanton where he bred horses to race and sell. Around the track he had a decent reputation. He spent necessary cash without groaning and his stock was honest and sometimes fairly good. Smart handicappers gave Nolan's starters an edge for condition and maybe talent. He employed a trainer, Steve Gardell, at the farm, and during Golden Gate meetings he always requisitioned a few stalls in which to board horses who'd be running regularly. This year he had three stalls and they were presided over by Debbie Thomas, a princess of the backstretch.

Debbie's official title was assistant trainer, but she spent most of her time grooming. The work showed in her body. Her shoulders were broad, her arms were hard and thickly muscled, and her hips were very trim. She had the build of a gymnast, somebody whose specialty was the parallel bars. She wore her blond hair at shoulder length and her eyes were blue and cool, except when she stepped outside the racetrack frame and became a young woman of twenty-two, pretty, a little dreamy, flirtatious, and decidedly feminine. She had three horses in her care: Ali Time, a dumb but honest two-year-old; Moonlight Cocktail, a moody filly; and Bushel Ruler, a handsome three-year-old gelding who hadn't raced yet. Of them all she loved only Bushel. She called him Oli, after his dam, Oligarch, and thought he'd fixated on her as a mother-substitute. When she walked down the shedrow in the morning, he'd stick his head out of the stall and whinny and nicker until she gave him some attention. He had personality and a touch of class, and Debbie wished she could change his name to something more suitable than Bushel Ruler.

Choosing the right name for a horse wasn't easy. The Jockey Club rules stated that you were limited to eighteen letters, counting spaces and punctuation, and couldn't duplicate names already registered or use those of "famous or notorious persons"—no Johnny Rotten, no Richard Nixon—or "trade names or names of commercial significance." Copyrighted names were permissible five years after their introduction into the culture, and so were "coined" and "made-up" names if they were accompanied by an explanation. There were also mystical injunctions to consider, like the Arabs' belief that a horse should never be named foolishly or in jest because he'd live up to that name. Language should be exact, as Dante once demonstrated to a Florentine blacksmith whom he caught reciting verses of *The Divine Comedy,* misquoting fiercely. Dante threw the man's hammer and tongs into the street, ruining them because the blacksmith had ruined his poetry. Debbie had once worked for a man who'd let her name all his horses, and she said the best names often came to her at night, in dreams. She was most proud of her choice for a colt out of Eskimo: *Chill Factor,* she'd called him, and it fit perfectly.

On the afternoon I met her, Debbie and Steve Gardell were preparing Moonlight Cocktail for the third race. Debbie said

Moony had always been a problem horse. She'd run so poorly the year before, once falling twenty lengths behind when favored, that everybody had written her off, but Nolan had shipped her to the veterinary school at the University of California, Davis, for a last-chance physical before turning her out. The vets took some X-rays and discovered a painful hoof disease, which they corrected. Now, Moony was on the comeback trail. During the Pacific meet she'd raced twice, but she was only beginning to round into shape. She was no longer crippled, just feisty, and Debbie bore the scars. Moony had kicked her twice, once in the leg and once in the head, breaking her nose and barely missing the critical space between her eyes. Every groom, and almost every trainer, told such tales, of hoofs flying out of nowhere to bunch an ear like cauliflower or scatter teeth like Chiclets, but I still found them harrowing. There was really nothing to protect you from the horses except a sort of grace conferred by the animals themselves.

Debbie knelt in the hay at the front of the stall and removed packed ice wrapped in towels from Moony's front legs. The ice kept the legs cool and the muscles tight. When the last ice shavings were brushed away, Gardell began wrapping the legs, applying cotton wads first, then Ace bandages sprinkled with paprika to keep the horse from chewing them loose, then wide swaths of adhesive tape. Taped front legs usually indicate that a horse has problems, but Debbie said in this instance the tape was cosmetic, meant to deceive. Moony was making a slight class drop, from eighty-five hundred to seventy-five hundred, and the bandages were supposed to plant a seed of doubt in any potential claimant's mind.

"She's got a real good chance to win," Debbie said. "She was real sharp when she galloped yesterday and I've been holding her off ever since. She's ready, if she's in the *mood* to run."

Later, I stood by the paddock fence and watched the third race entries as they circled. Flowering bushes along the perimeter of the paddock gave off a soapy smell from white waxen blooms, and I had the impression that the horses had all been recently bathed. Moony looked splendid. She had green ribbons laced into her mane, and her dark brown coat had a fine sheen. Her quarters were tight and had a sculptural intensity, a focusing of power, and as she walked she kept her ears pricked. Debbie had also dressed for the occasion, in a Western shirt, a leather belt decorated with blue flowers and a pair of new jeans. Her hair was brushed and she wore sunglasses. She stood very erect, conscious of her posture, and she whispered constantly to Moony as they circled. Their heads seemed confined to a single plane and they moved forward as a unit. Seeing Debbie so brushed up and shiny made me aware of the plight of less presentable grooms. Some of them hated the paddock, its public nature, the way it accentuated their pimples and boils, and though they did their best to clean up and face it squarely they always looked like recalcitrant children sent off to school. They had too much oil in their hair, bloody shaving nicks on their cheeks, and creases in shirts and blouses badly folded and stored too long in musty bottom drawers. That the world valued beauty, and rewarded it disproportionately, was never so apparent as in the paddock.

I went to the windows, still smelling soap, and bet the selection I'd made the night before. Moonlight Cocktail chose to run and won by a half-length, closing fast and paying $14.20.

VI

Though I hadn't yet learned to distinguish hot tips from cool ones, I was learning other things about handicapping at Golden Gate Fields. On hot days when the track baked to an unyielding consistency the color of pie crust, I looked for front-runners because their speed seemed to last and they weren't so easily caught from behind. On foggy days the track was heavy and moist, deep and dark as chocolate, and then I looked for horses who'd been running in the Northwest, at Longacres near Seattle or Oregon's Portland Meadows, because they were used to heavy strips and often ran better than the *Form* indicated they might. I stopped betting any exacta race in which the favorite went off at less than eight to five because, for reasons inexplicable to me, these races almost never ran to form. I quit playing the ninth altogether because it was another exacta, the fourth of the day, a crazy last chance for bettors to win back what they'd lost; the Racing Secretary usually carded a long route, a mile and an eighth, a mile and a quarter, and the jockeys often rode in such a controlled and controlling fashion that the outcome was more than a little suspect.

But my major insight to date was something I called the Bandit Syndrome. It occurred most frequently in maiden claiming races and involved horses who'd done poorly at Hollywood Park or Santa Anita and had been shipped to Golden Gate for the express purpose of breaking their maidens against cheaper competition. These horses *robbed* their victories, and when I noticed their presence I was often able to cash in. The most flagrant example of the syndrome I ever witnessed took place one balmy afternoon, when a Ross Brinson–trained filly, Miss Raedine, was entered in a sprint for two-year-olds. Though her past performance charts showed that she got out of the gate well, she'd faded badly in both her starts, finishing fifth and then sixth by eleven lengths. I bet her heavily to win, reminding myself that she'd been running against the best stock in the nation. With five minutes to go her odds began to drop and by post time she was down to two to one. Approaching the gate she suddenly became fractious and threw her rider, Bill Mahorney, then slipped past the handlers and sprinted the wrong way down the backstretch, her mane flying, until a ponyboy headed her and, as in a roundup, herded her back to post. This unscheduled romp would've drained most horses and knocked them out of contention, but Miss Raedine was raring to go. Mahorney dusted himself off, boarded her again—again she tried to unseat him—held on tight while the handlers pushed her into the slot and then boomed out in a manic burst of speed when the gate flapped open. The next morning I read the *Form's* chart of the race and it made me feel good inside.

Horse	Eqt.	A.	Wt	PP	St	¼	⅜	Str	Fin	Jockey	Cl'g Pr	Odds $1
Miss Raedine		2	117	3	3	1^2	1^2	1^5	1^1	Mahorney W	12500	2.30
Ribo Glen		2	117	5	7	$6^{1\frac12}$	5^2	$2^{\frac12}$	2^1	Ramirez O	12500	24.80
Shady Re		2	117	4	8	8^1	7^2	$4^{1\frac12}$	$3^{1\frac12}$	Schacht R	12500	15.20
Safesilver		2	117	10	2	$3^{\frac12}$	3^2	$3^{1\frac12}$	4^{hd}	Gomez R	12500	7.20
Fiji Honey		2	117	7	1	5^2	4^{hd}	5^4	5^4	Aragon J	12500	9.00
Summer Living		2	117	2	10	$7^{1\frac12}$	$6^{1\frac12}$	7^2	6^1	Munoz E	12500	45.20
Lowengren		2	117	9	9	10	9^6	8^5	7^5	Gonzalez R M	12500	2.80
Country Beat	b	2	112	6	5	4^1	8^1	9^6	8^2	Galarsa R^5	12500	12.70
Happy as a Lark		2	117	8	4	$2^{1\frac12}$	2^3	6^2	9^4	Noguez A M	12500	27.90
Handy Pocket		2	117	1	6	9^1	10	10	10	Wilburn J	12500	4.40

OFF AT 12:36 PDT. Start good. Won driving. Time; :22⅖, :46⅗, :59⅘, 1:06⅗ Track fast.

Official Program Numbers

	3 Miss Raedine	6.60	4.20	3.80
$2 Mutuel Prices:	5 Ribo Glen		17.80	11.20
	4 Shady Re			7.60

B. f, by Vested Power—KoKodera, by Creme dela Creme. Trainer Brinson Ross. Bred by Winchell V H Jr (Cal).

VII

Late in April Headley gave Pichi her first start of the year in a maiden race to be run at six furlongs for a purse of six thousand dollars. He engaged Jane Driggers to ride and she wore the Sandomirs' colors, yellow and black stripes topped with a black cap. Pichi drew the outermost post, twelve, which wasn't as disadvantageous as it seemed. She lugged in toward the rail, listing always to the left, so she'd at least be as far away as possible from that particular problem. Whether it would influence her performance was unclear. Bettors shied from her in great numbers, depositing their money instead on Sailing Flag, who'd been bred in Kentucky and had some Fleet Nasrullah blood, and letting Pichi go off at eighty-five to one. Sentiment overtook me and I put two dollars on her nose.

She behaved well in the gate, much to Headley's relief, and broke well too, second after the buzzer, but she got into trouble immediately, blocked by other horses, and dropped back into the pack and disappeared. A speedy filly named Hut's Girl took command, and according to the *Form's* subsequent description, "proved much the best under intermittent urging," winning by eight lengths and leaving Sailing Flag unfurled in the dust. Pichi finished eighth, fifteen lengths behind, but she did make a tiny move in the stretch, expending a minuscule atom of acceleration, and gained a little ground. Her showing, while not a cause for celebration, wasn't nearly as bad as Exclusive Delight's, who trailed the pack and fashioned a running line that read like a numerological rendering of oblivion, 12-12-12-12, last at every point of call. I saw Headley after the race and expected him to be shattered, his long months of conditioning proven worthless, but on the contrary he seemed pleased and promised better things from Pichi in the future. "I told you she'd need a race," he said. "You watch her next time out." *Hope,* I thought, that's what you purchase at eighty-five to one.

Before the next race I fell victim to confusion once again. I was torn between the rational order of things and my intuition and what it proposed. A sensible reading of the *Form* had convinced me to play Top Delegate, who'd been running well against allowance-class company and was dropping down to his proper level, but I kept returning to another horse, Little Shasta, because the name reminded me of Mount Shasta and the fine trout waters around it. Names could be irresistible. I remembered the time my brother and I had rented a boat and tooled across Lake Shasta and then up into an arm of the Pit River, where we camped for the night. We were fresh from Long Island, still unused to the sight of mountains, and our only camping experience was of the backyard pup-tent variety. At dusk we heard howling in the foothills, a wild blood-chilling sound that increased after dark. "A killer dog," I said. "You're right," said my brother, and we broke camp immediately and slept in the boat, anchored safely some fifty yards from shore. It had only been a coyote howling, but I didn't realize this until much later when the call had become familiar. So Little Shasta spoke to me of innocence, of lakes and wildness and pines and the few things in life I'd come finally to know. On the other hand, Top Delegate reminded me of Henry Kissinger, and I was fighting this associational bias all the way to the windows. I got into line and while scanning my program I noticed that Little Shasta's post position, four, corresponded to the number the boy with the bass had given me at San Pablo Reservoir. Suddenly I was face to face with a ruddy-skinned ticket seller in a black cardigan sweater. "Eight," I said and then watched in misery as Little Shasta went wire to wire, winning as decidedly as Pichi had lost.

Every now and then the structural pattern was broken by instances of pure vision, gifts, and I kept rejecting them, time and again. Arnold Walker understood. I bumped into him at the bar at Spenger's. "You're not talking about luck," he said, chewing on a swizzle stick. "That's when you win because the horse in front of your horse falls down and breaks a leg."

"What *am* I talking about?"

"What you're talking about is magic. When your horse is the *only* horse in the race."

VIII

Later that night I found myself in a Berkeley "repertory cinema" with torn seats and atmospheric reefer smoke, watching a low-budget horror movie, *Tarantula.* Giant spiders were taking over the earth. They did all sorts of damage in the process, but their peregrinations were as difficult to handicap as those of horses. One day they'd eat a city and the next be gone, returned to secretive arachnoid plotting down in filthy earthen caverns. For a while it looked as though they might succeed in ridding the planet of humans and vegetation, so troublesome were they to detect. When the film's heroine, Mara Corday, threw up her hands and announced disgustedly, "Well, I've had enough of the Unknown for *one* afternoon," I felt the beating of a kindred spirit within her breast and thought I might run into her when I stopped in at the Home Stretch for a nightcap. She wasn't there, but I stayed anyway, right until closing time, cleansing my mind of spiders and thoroughbreds. When I got back to the Terrace, all the rooms were pleasantly still and the air smelled of tar and gasoline, the urban essence of spring. I sat on the steps by my door, wanting to talk to somebody. I thought about calling my wife but she would be asleep and the woman who operated the motel switchboard would also be asleep. Almost everybody was asleep, even the horses. I should've gone to bed myself, but instead I sat on the steps and thought about the Unknown and realized that I was pushing at the track, still trying too hard. My disappointment came from expectations, from proposing a shape for the experience I was seeking and then feeling let down when the experience arrived in a shape other than the one I'd proposed.

The Unknown had only been doing its job, existing as a trans-
formative condition—not an end-stopped province like the future
—and delivering me to the cusp of mysteries. I had a terrific
urge to get into the car and drive through the streets until I'd
found Mara, or her image, and share my revelations, which
would give her the courage necessary to face the spiders again,
but this urge escaped, too, with the slacking of heat and the first
sloughing-off of spent brain cells.

IX

In the morning I didn't want to see Mara Corday. I ate a breakfast of mammoth cholesterolic proportions and eased my con-
science with Plato. God gave us the lower belly and bowels as a
safeguard against intemperance, the philosopher said, so that we
wouldn't be destroyed by disease before our mortal race had ful-
filled its end, whatever that was. I went to the track and locked
all my money in the glove compartment. Being cashless, and
hence without portfolio, seemed to free my eyes and I saw many
wondrous things: horses quitting at the head of the stretch, horses
racing wide or lugging in, perfectly positioned horses failing to
respond when asked, horses going wildly off stride, and Big
Bruiser pulling up lame in the ninth, a fitting close. An awesome
randomness was on view. At the clubhouse bar, I ran into a
trainer of my acquaintance. His face was splotched, his eyes were
·bleary, and in his fist he held a wad of crushed exacta tickets. It
took a long time for him to speak, and when he did his boozy
voice soughed like the wind.

"I gave that horse everything he could want," the trainer said,
"and look what the bastard went and did to me." He let go of
the tickets, several hundred dollars' worth, and they fluttered to
the floor.

Even princes, Machiavelli thought, were subject to the vagaries of fortune. It was good to be adventurous and embody the primary virtues, but someday, inevitably, the river would rise and wash away trees, buildings, plans, and schemes. "All yield to its violence, without being able in any way to withstand it; and yet, though its nature be such, it does not follow therefore that men, when the weather becomes fair, shall not make provision, both with defenses and barriers, in such a manner that, rising again, the waters may pass away by canal, and their force be neither so unrestrained or so dangerous." This struck me as an accurate metaphor for the work of trainers. It was canal work they did, an attempt at channeling energies beyond their control, but they were only intermittently successful. The pulse kept its own rhythm, somewhere deep inside.

Chapter Five

The cripples always amazed me, there were so many of them. They arrived early, well before the first race, and were wheeled or otherwise assisted across the parking lot and then past the three hucksters selling mimeographed sucker sheets. A tall radish-cheeked man sold Bob's card, and a man whose skin was almost cream-colored sold Bull's, but they were generally ignored in favor of the unsavory man in a trench coat who was stationed closest to the door. *"Hoymet!"* the man cried, picking at his chin, "Hoymet heah, five winnahs yestahday, Hoymet has da double for ya," and the cripples reached into their pockets and donated a dollar for the Hermit's daily words of wisdom. They were plentiful, these words, because the Hermit usually offered two selections in every race and threw in five combinations for the daily double, as well as a smattering of exacta numbers and exacta suggestions and long-shot exactas, below which, in bold block letters, the following cautionary sentence was printed: TANFORAN RACING ASSN. DOESN'T SPONSOR THESE SELECTIONS.

Inside, the cripples stationed themselves along the clubhouse rail, their wheelchairs lined up near the finish line, and began quietly sorting through their materials: *Forms,* programs, suggestions clipped from the daily papers, and the sucker sheets. They had a dignity about them, a stillness that remained undisturbed even as the action around them increased. While watching them assemble I thought of their ranks, of all our ranks, being duplicated at racetracks across the land. Every day twenty-six thousand of us descended on Santa Anita, ten thousand more stopped in at Calder in Florida, and another twenty-one thousand made their deposits at Oak Lawn Park. Even the poorest tracks had a following—four thousand a day at Latonia in Kentucky and a thousand at little Rillito Downs in Arizona. Many greenbacks made the rounds; four million dollars would be handled at Santa Anita alone. In a given year we'd watch some sixty-nine thousand races, in which sixty-two thousand horses would start a total of six hundred thousand times for purses totaling three hundred thirty-six million.

A short fat man breezed by, on his way to cash in a winning ticket from the previous day. "You see that race?" he asked. "Our Star Chuck? The one who paid a hundred fifty? I had that horse." He showed me the ticket, grasping it protectively between his thumb and index finger. "I rode in with this guy, he's not even a friend of mine, really, but his name's Chuck, so for the hell of it when he bought a ticket on the horse I bought one, too. Then the horse comes in. I couldn't believe it. The horse came in. Twenty-seven years I'm handicapping, I never once hit a big winner. Not once. Then the horse comes in. I couldn't believe it. So that's how it happens, I said. I think my hair was standing up. I couldn't believe it. Hell with this, I said, went out, sat in the car the rest of the afternoon."

In the men's room the stalls were all occupied by students, clipboards balanced on their knees, and an old guy with ratbreath was washing his dentures in the sink. "I was born in Wichita," he said. "My mother was a Cree. She never touched alcohol. It made her crazy. I love racing but if I ever win any money I'm going back to Kansas. If you don't believe me you can ask Don."

Riding down the elevator I studied the toupees on display, the worst I'd ever seen, worse even than those in burlesque houses or on the TV weathermen in small towns. They inspired disbelief. These were clown rugs, the kind of mustard-colored mats that were plastered to heads, then whisked away by fishing hooks or blown sky-high by studio wind machines. Stunning polyester and doubleknit ensembles were also on parade, the Spiegel catalog come to life. A young man with a wolfman pompadour and an expensive but tasteless suit was putting the make on a classically cheap-speed blonde. "I went to Vegas over the weekend," he said. "You know Wayne Newton? The singer? I hang out with his bodyguard's brother-in-law."

Turnstiles were clicking briskly down on the ground level, where people strode determinedly off buses from Oakland, Richmond, and San Francisco as though they'd been promised a big slice of Transformation Pie and couldn't wait to bite into it. "I dreamed the numbers last night," said a balding lady in a heavy fur coat and mittens. "Four and six, clear as could be, only I never did dream what race they was in. Going to cost me twenty dollar to find out. Be worth it, though. Last week, one exacta, it paid a thousand dollar. A thousand dollar. I said *a thousand dollar!* You know how long it take me to make that kind of money?"

Upstairs members of special groups were being led to their tables in the special groups' section near the Turf Club. Most of them had never been to the track before, or maybe just once during the Second World War when Uncle George rolled into town and dragged everybody to Bay Meadows, and as they picked their seats they seemed openly thrilled by the excitement at hand, the *raciness* of racing. They lived in bedroom communities and were dressed simply unless they belonged to a group that believed in funny hats or badges or other emblematic attire, and they would spend the afternoon eating and drinking and betting on pretty horses and long shots. One of them—it was impossible to say at the outset *which* one—would win a hundred dollars and become an addict. "It started at Golden Gate," he would say later, "over creamed chicken on toast." Management took good care of special groups and named a purse in honor of each of them: Rotary Club of Piedmont Purse, Nomads of Santa Rosa Purse, Women in Construction Purse, R.J.'s Cocktail Lounge Purse, Fashionettes Social Club Purse, Standard Oil Wives Purse, NARF Fun Groupe Purse, and Mary and Bob Franchetto's Fortieth Birthday Party Purse.

Right after the national anthem, the black kids who seemed to live under the paddock got ready to work. There were three or four of them, streetwise jivey kids with hair done in cornrows and dreadlocks, and each day they staked out a square of macadam directly below the runway leading from the Jockeys' Room to the paddock. When jockeys strolled down the runway before a race, the kids were *on their case* immediately, hooking fingers through the chain-link fence and pulling themselves onto the concrete ledge and beginning their interrogation.

"Hey, Mahoney," they yelled at Bill Mahorney, who walked the runway like a condemned man, as though a thirty-pound weight had been embedded between his shoulder blades, "you gonna give that horse a ride today? You gonna ride him right? What about that horse, Mahoney? He sound? He feelin' all right? Last time out he was limpin', Mahoney. C'mon, tell the truth, don't be lyin' to me now." Most jockeys stared off into space, but a few seemed to enjoy the exchange. " 'Rique, my man, hey there, Muñoz, hey, *'Rique* my *man,* you gonna get that horse out of the gate this time? I'm askin' now, 'Rique, you dig? 'Cause if you don't get him out, that sucker don't stand a chance. Aw, don't be makin' faces, 'Rique, you can talk to *me*." Every once in a while they charmed a jockey, one who knew what it was like, and the jockey winked or muttered a few syllables out of the corner of his mouth and the kids ran off to bet. We were all pilgrims in our way.

II

I sat by the Terrace swimming pool, reading about magic. A salesman from an educational publishing company sat in the chair next to mine. I'd met him earlier when he'd caught me staring into his car, a late-model Pontiac with a back seat full of globes, spheres of reinforced cardboard, blue, green, and brown, spilled into a tangle of equatorial seat belts. The sight was marvelous, and not a little unexpected, and I lingered, staring, until the salesman came out of his room and asked me what the hell I was doing. The globes had overwhelmed me, I said, and then showed him my room key to prove I wasn't a thief. This made him feel guilty. Minor judgmental errors tend to unhinge men who've been drinking alone in motel rooms since two in the afternoon. He opened the trunk of his car and insisted on giving me an outdated model he'd collected from a Berkeley retailer. "Keep it, keep it," he said. "I already credited the guy's account. Company can't use it." He tapped the globe with a finger. "Africa's all screwed up. They keep changing the names over there."

I put the globe on my dresser and as a fair-trade gesture gave the man—Ted—a warm beer from my stash on the windowsill, which was a mistake. When I went to sit by the pool Ted joined me, bringing along an ice bucket, two sani-sealed glasses, and a half-bottle of Old Stasis bourbon. He wanted to get a little snock-ered and then go looking for "nookie," but I was after the magic and couldn't explain. So we sat together and listened to the ice melt. It melted slowly, with no audible variation. Finally Ted got to his feet and pulled up his trousers, which seemed to con-tain thousands of pennies, and said, "Well, I better turn in. Got to be in Palo Alto early tomorrow." We shook hands and he made me write my name and address on the back of his business card so he could send me an atlas, *gratis,* when he got home to Citrus Heights, some horrible planned community near Sacra-mento. The atlas has yet to arrive.

III

In 1460 a Macedonian monk brought Cosimo de' Medici a manu-script reputed to be an incomplete copy of the secret, magical *Corpus Hermeticum,* a book supposedly written by Thoth, the Egyptian god of wisdom, who was known to the Florentines by his Greek name, Hermes Trismegistus. Hermes was held in high regard for his powers and valued, as were many things during the Renaissance, for his antiquity. He predated Plato, for whom Cosimo had forsaken Aristotle, and hence was considered *prima materia,* closer to the flame. Cosimo was old and sick and wanted to read the *Corpus,* even in fragmentary form, before he died, so he repaired to his villa above Florence and summoned court scholar Marsilio Ficino.

"I arrived here at Careggi yesterday," he wrote Ficino in his letter of instruction, "not in order to till my fields, but to cultivate my soul."

Ficino came at once. He was a short serious melancholy man who'd established his reputation as a translator early in life, while still at school. Cosimo had made him a ward of the Medici so he could translate, for Cosimo's delectation, Plato's work from Greek into Latin without being subjected to the usual distractions of penurious scholars. For Ficino the arrangement was a windfall. Since his youth he'd been devoted to Plato and to the notion that love in its idealized Platonic form was the universe's glue, its sustaining principle; Cosimo's patronage gave him the freedom to try to reconcile such doctrines with those of the Church. Religion and philosophy were both spiritual pursuits, he believed, and it was his desire to fuse his own mystical Platonism with the conceptual core of Christianity. To this end he labored on in a villa near Cosimo's, under the blank marble stare of a bust of Plato that Cosimo had given him. Once a year, on Plato's birthday, Ficino held a banquet for leading statesmen, artists, writers, and students, the nucleus of his informal "Academy." Arriving guests, tired from the long journey on horseback, up from the city into hills leavened with vines and olive trees, were instructed to take note of the motto Ficino had inscribed (perhaps as a caution against the weight of his own humors) on a wall of the villa: FREE TROUBLES, BE HAPPY IN THE PRESENT.

At Cosimo's request, Ficino set aside his other work and took up the fragments of the *Corpus*. He recognized the importance of the find; only Zoroaster came before Hermes in the genealogy of wisdom. By 1463 Ficino had finished a translation, Greek to Latin. This he presented to Cosimo, who was almost on his deathbed. The *Corpus* was something of a disappointment, though, at least in its philosophical sections, which only echoed the longings and aspirations of Humanism. In one characteristic passage, Pimander, an aspect of the Divine Mind, floats down to earth to give dozing Hermes advice on conducting his life. Man's doubleness complicates existence, Pimander says; your flesh is mortal, but you are immortal by connection to essential man. Unlike other creatures, man can grow and change and perhaps become one with the Divine Mind. "You are light and life, like God the Father of whom Man was born. If therefore you know yourself as made of light and life . . . you will return to life." This was familiar stuff, but the magical elements in the *Corpus* excited Ficino and his friends and helped to liberate the figure of the magus from the granite and doxology of the medieval church.

Before the advent of Christianity, and through the period of its inception and diaspora, magicians had flourished in and around Florence. They were consulted not only for potions and abracadabras, but for the medicinal herbs, roots, and barks that formed the substance of the early pharmacy. But priests were afraid of them and believed that they practiced a form of black magic designed to topple the Church, so a campaign against them was mounted and they were forced underground. The *Corpus* helped to redefine magic and broaden the scope of its praxis. There were really *two* categories of magic, black and white, malevolent and benevolent, and Hermes advocated the use of a variety of the latter, called *sympathetic*.

According to the scholar Francis Yates, this magic worked by *simpatia,* sympathy, by "knowing the mutual reports running through all nature, the secret charms by which one thing can be drawn to another." It explored affinities and relationships and tried to attract celestial energy, *spiritus,* and then deploy it in the service of benign goals. Pico pushed this distinction even further. He described sympathetic magic as "the utter perfection of natural philosophy," hardly magical at all, and certainly separate from that other magic "which depends entirely on the work and authority of demons, a thing to be abhorred, so help me the God of truth, and a monstrous thing." Even the word *magus* had been misconstrued, Pico wrote. In fact it derived from Persian and "expresses the same idea as 'interpreter' and 'worshipper

of the divine' with us." Pico's naive reformulation, sure to appeal
to academics, did much to enhance magic's reputation, and soon
magical texts of all sorts, translations as well as newly written
materials, were in great demand. Ficino contributed a volume
called *On Capturing the Life of the Stars*. It was an eclectic
compendium, somewhat like an herbal, full of imaginative pre-
scriptions for healing body and soul.

An Arabian manual, *Picatrix,* had influenced Ficino's work
and portions of it were quoted in the book I was reading. There
was a long description of a city Hermes/Thoth had built in
Egypt and controlled by manipulating images.

On the eastern gate he placed the form of an Eagle; on the
western gate, the form of a Bull; on the southern gate the form
of a Lion, and on the northern gate the form of a Dog. Into
these images he introduced spirits which spoke with voices, nor
could anyone enter the gates of the City except by their permis-
sion. There he planted trees in the midst of which was a great
tree which bore the fruit of all generation. On the summit of
the castle he caused to be raised a tower thirty cubits high on
the top of which he ordered to be placed a light-house the
colour of which changed every day until the seventh day after
which it returned to the first colour, and so the City was il-
luminated with these colours. Near the City there was an
abundance of waters in which dwelt many kinds of fish. Around
the circumference of the City he placed engraved images and
ordered them in such a manner that by virtue of it the in-
habitants were made virtuous and withdrawn from all wicked-
ness and harm. The name of the City was Adocentyn.

The description had a fairy-tale piquancy, and that night I
dreamed of Adocentyn. It was still with me in the morning when
I went to the track.

IV

The race was for two-year-olds, a five-furlong sprint, and I looked over the stock in the paddock before making my wager. The horses had run only once or twice before, or not at all, and they were still green and had the alert playful look of the ranch about them. They weren't aware of resistances, opposition, the gradual wearing down of tissue and desire, and some of them had a bafflement in their eyes when they surveyed the grandstand and the unfamiliar faces reading their limbs. I liked to bet two-year-olds because they were so young and guileless. Older horses, the *Form*'s "hard-hitting veterans," were often deceptive before a race, drag-assing around, shuffling, their backs swayed and noses dappling the dust, and more than once I'd lost money when just such an animal rose into himself a hundred yards from the gate, suddenly pumped up on thoroughbred afflatus, and led the field from wire to wire.

Two horses in the present field attracted me, Pass Completion, the favorite, and an outsider, Flight Message. Both looked honest, and I was standing in front of a toteboard, trying to decide between them, when an old man came up and asked if he could look at my *Form*. He was very polite, with clean pink cheeks, and he smelled of cologne and a dash of clubhouse whiskey and wore gold-rimmed specs and a traditional senior citizen's shirt, white nylon and short-sleeved, with a strapped T-shirt beneath it.

"Haven't read one of these for years," he mumbled, running the spine of his comb under lines of type. "Say, this horse *has* been working well. Raindrop Kid. Raindrop Kid. What're the odds?" he asked, squinting.

"Eighteen to one."

"Eighteen to one? Eighteen to one?" His eyes were gleaming now and a bit of froth appeared on his lips. "That's an overlay if ever I saw one," he said before vanishing into the six-dollar-combination line.

Around me people were suddenly moving, prodded into action by the five-minute-warning buzzer, and I was arrested by the swarming colors and shapes, nests of teased hair, lime-green trousers, dark skin. I wondered if the old man knew what he was talking about or if he was just another trailer-park baron on holiday. It occurred to me that he might be a manifestation, some emissary from the outposts of my consciousness. I looked around. He wasn't there. Time was passing, so I stepped into the flow to play Pass Completion, but when I reached for my money, I pulled out something along with it, a small antique medal my brother had given me years ago. I'd used it as a key chain until the hook at the top had broken, and now I carried it for sentimental reasons. It pictured a knickered boy in a golf cap rolling up his sleeves and preparing to flick a marble at other marbles arranged in a cruciform at the center of a circle. Above the boy's head were the words, "United States Marble Shooting Championship Tournament." His feet rested on laurel leaves. There was no illustration on the other side, only text: "Malden Championship Awarded to Emil Lawrence by *The Boston Traveler*," it read. Nowhere did it mention Adocentyn, but I still bet Raindrop Kid to win.

Sometimes a race unfolds exactly as you've envisioned it, with the horses cleaving to a pattern in your brain, and this seemed to be happening now. Raindrop Kid broke slowly, as I thought he would, and was seventh at the three-sixteenths pole, but I expected him to begin moving soon and he did, on the outside. By the stretch he was in striking distance. His legs were fully extended and he moved along in an effortless coltish glide. He trailed My Golly, whom I hadn't even considered, and as he drew up to challenge I waited for the next phase of the pattern to develop, horses hooked and matching stride for stride, and then the final phase, the Kid's slick expenditure of energy he'd held in reserve, his head thrown forward just far enough to nip My Golly at the wire. But it was My Golly who began to accelerate, drawing away, and I watched him pass the finish line and felt the pattern dissolve, soup draining into my shoes.

Then the "Inquiry" sign appeared on the toteboard. The stewards were going to review a videotape of the race because my jockey, Rogelio Gomez, had lodged a complaint against Enrique Muñoz on My Golly, claiming Muñoz had bumped him in the stretch. The sign had a strange effect on me. It was one turnaround too many and I felt unpleasantly suspended. I turned away and looked up and saw a sparrow trying to pin a moth against the windbreak of the grandstand. The ongoing business of biology made me aware of the sound of my heart and the blood circulating through my body. I took a deep breath, but the air was warm and settled miasmatically in my lungs. Somebody had spilled popcorn down the steps in front of me, and for a while I counted kernels. The waiting was bad, as it always is, and I tried thinking about other things. The man next to me had a digital watch strapped to his wrist and I wondered how such instruments would affect our sense of time, extracting numbers from some bottomless well instead of graphing them, as clock hands did, across a recognizable globe. Computers with their miniaturized functions had a tendency to destroy space by making it seem equivalent to time, of the same invisible substance, when in fact the opposite was true: space was real, was grass, trees, rivers, and earth, real as horses are and so of greater validity than human constructs like time.

A sudden explosion of bulbs, brilliant flashes on the toteboard, interrupted my cogitation, and then John Gibson, the track announcer, announced in that grand theatrical manner he had, full of hesitations, that after examining the videotape . . . the stewards . . . had decided . . . to *disqualify* My Golly and award the race to Raindrop Kid. The Kid paid thirty-eight dollars and twenty cents for every two dollars wagered to win, and when I collected my money I could feel the heat in my hands, all through me, and I knew how hot I was going to get.

V

John Gibson's booth, which looks like a fishing shack on the fringe of some desperate hyacinth-choked lake, is on the roof of the grandstand, and to get to it I had to ascend a secret staircase behind a bar in the special groups' dining room. It was a windy day and I could feel the grandstand trembling under my feet. The tenuousness of the structure was apparent. It seemed almost to list from left to right in concord with the gusting winds. I could see across the Bay to San Francisco, where a fire was burning on the Embarcadero. Dark gray smoke funneled into the sky and from where I stood, miles away, it looked beautiful, robbed of its tragic elements. Chaos, too, was a shifting notion, a matter of perspective, and I thought Gibson's job must be a difficult one because nine times a day he had to lend a sense of order and purpose to animals spilling out of the gate. This was Gibson's first season at Golden Gate, his first ever calling thoroughbreds—he'd had some experience with trotters and pacers at Hollywood Park, but that was a simpler business—and he was having a little trouble adjusting. Every announcer puts the wrong horse in front sometimes, but Gibson made the mistake frequently and had on occasion named the wrong horse at the wire. His style was imitative of Harry Henson's, the dean of Hollypark, and his tongue didn't easily embrace the foreign syllables fate tossed his way. Certain horses might never have their names pronounced right, not by Gibson, but then again he was young, only twenty-seven, and had plenty of time to improve.

Inside, the booth was crammed with chairs, shelves, electronic equipment that an engineer named Charlie used to tape and later feed delayed race calls to KCBS in San Francisco, soda cans, beer cans, plates scarred with dried gravy, cake and pie plates tumbling crumbs—Gibson was a big man, pushing three hundred pounds—books and magazines, Gibson himself, and the track electrician, Ernie, a shifty-eyed man who was busy repairing a battery-powered horse-racing game. Ernie flipped a switch, testing, and the little horses, pushed forward by vibrations, began jiggling along their slots toward a finish line about ten inches away.

"Red horse is still too fast," Ernie said.

"We're gonna have to heavy-weight that sucker," said Gibson. He took a thin strand of wire and wrapped it around the base of the horse. "That ought to slow 'im down."

Gibson liked games and used them to fill up the dead time between races. He had something called Space Shuttle, which involved maneuvering a steel ball with two steel rods toward a hole at the end of a wooden board, but his favorite was darts. His dart board was nailed to the far wall, above Charlie's equipment, and because Gibson was fairly inept it was dangerous for Charlie to let his attention lag. When Gibson was throwing, darts bounced all over the shack, skewering *Form*s and forearms alike. He lost two quick games to Ernie, who seemed to be toying with him, and then took me to an elevated platform at the front of the booth. This was where he worked. He sat on a stool with a microphone around his neck and used high-powered binoculars to scan the track. The view was exceptional, with nothing but glass between him and the strip.

Gibson's calling problems were due mostly to inexperience. His flaws seemed exaggerated, though, because he'd been hired to replace a local favorite, Tod Creed, who had resigned in a dispute with management. Creed, Berkeley-born, talented, with the high-strung temperament of a diva, was legendary for his fits, fights, and outbursts. Often he got away with them because he was so good at what he did. Over the years he'd been offered jobs at several major-league tracks but had chosen to stay close to home and his aging mother and boyhood pals. When he walked into Spenger's, he was greeted with enthusiasm. Waiters slapped him on the back and bartenders filled his wineglass without being asked and said, winking, "On the house, Toddy, it's on the house."

Creed was expert at many aspects of calling, but his greatest strength was in playing the crowd. An announcer has to work on fans, to build the pace of a race with his voice, wheedling and modulating and creating effects, and then at the finish punch it to them in a vibrant hoof-echoing staccato. Creed could do this splendidly. He loved to joke, and he'd take a rider's name and stretch it out like taffy, Raul Caballero, taking the syllables in Raul apart, then reassembling them as a wolflike howl, Ra-*oooool,* his voice keening, going after those frail high notes just off the scale, and then he'd follow it up with a rumpitythump letter-perfect Spanish rendition of Caballero, the aptest surname on the backstretch. The jockeys liked Creed for buffing their stars and also for his concern over their safety. If a horse broke down during a race, Creed alerted the riders, and if the situation was really bad, portending an accident, he'd take it upon himself to stop the race entirely, shouting, "Pull up, jockeys, pull up, this race is over." Management didn't approve of such usurpations, but Creed wouldn't be swayed. In the booth he was Caesar. You can do strange things with a microphone, he liked to say. The most difficult part of calling a race, he said, wasn't sorting out the horses after the break but picking them up when they came out of the first turn. The image you saw flipflopped then, going from side-view to head-view, and the worst mistakes were made.

But everybody missed one occasionally. Creed told me once about the time he was calling a night race at Cahokia Downs in St. Louis with a dense tule fog obscuring the track and the yellow arc lights giving the proceedings an infernal glow. Two jockeys in the race were wearing blue silks. One rode an even-money favorite, the other a fifty-to-one shot. In the fog Creed mixed them up and had the fifty-to-one shot winning, when in fact the favorite had crossed the wire first. A minute later he corrected himself, but the damage was already done. Angry fans who held tickets on the long shot were demanding Creed's head on a pole—he'd nearly doled out several coronaries—and one of them, a giant, materialized at the door of the booth, apparently to rip Creed to pieces. But the giant's anger fizzled when he saw Creed's dark-tinted glasses. Instead of hitting Creed, he groaned and slapped his forehead.

"I *knew* they must've had a blind man in here," he said.

Gibson had avoided any physical confrontations so far. As a rule he left Golden Gate right after the ninth race and drove nearly a hundred miles to his home in a Sacramento River delta town, close to *his* birthplace, where he could relax and do a little striped bass fishing. He used threadfin shad for bait and had a special method for rigging them, running a wire from mouth to tail to keep them on the hook longer. There was nothing quite so tasty as fresh striped bass, Gibson said, fried or cooked on a grill, and then he tugged on the brim of his porkpie hat and stepped onto the viewing platform for the next race. He reviewed the horses running, pronouncing the names over and over again. "Tiercel," he said, consulting Charlie and Ernie, "are we making that Ter-cel or *Tear*-cel?" He memorized post positions and silks colors, and at Ernie's suggestion performed a little of the old Spike Jones racetrack routine, "It's Cabbage by a head, Carrot by a nose," and so on, until the horses left the paddock. "Just five minutes until post time, ladies and gentlemen," he said. It was odd to stand next to him and hear the familiar sentence and not feel prodded into the usual last-minute scurrying. "I'll tell you one thing," Gibson said, "if you want to be an announcer you better start when you're about fifteen or you won't get anywhere." He picked up his binoculars and focused them. "I'm not kidding you," he said.

VI

So Gibson fished for stripers, as did Slaughterhouse Red and the grooms and some of the jockeys, and Creed fished for trout, up in the Sierras, and Bob Hack fished whenever he got a chance. Optimism, pursuit of slippery creatures, the desire to connect with forces beyond your control. Driving back to the Terrace one evening I passed a backwater slough growing spiky reeds and long fingers of grass, perfect habitat for catfish, and thought, *I bet there's horses in there.*

VII

All week long I kept winning. It had nothing to do with systems, I was just *in touch*. When I walked through the grandstand I projected the winner's aura, blue and enticing. Women smiled openly as I passed. I drank good whiskey and ate well. One night I went to a Japanese restaurant and sat at a table opposite Country Joe Macdonald, the singer who'd been a fixture at rallies in the sixties. Joe had a new wife with him, and a new baby who refused to sit still and instead bawled and threw an order of *sushi* around the room. A chunk of tuna flew past my ear. Even this seemed revelatory, the domestic roundness of a star's life, his interrupted meal, carrying the baby crying into the night, and I knew that someday soon Tuna or Seaweed or Rice-ball would appear on the menu at Golden Gate and I'd play the horse and win. Things fleshed themselves out before my eyes. In a liquor store I bought two bottles of Sapporo Black and went to sit on the Terrace steps and listen to my upstairs neighbor's piano exercises, the dusky fastnesses of ivory. This tune, I thought, will never end.

VIII

One morning as I stood by the rail I saw Debbie Thomas gal-loping Bushel Ruler. He looked good coming through the fog, the edges of his body softened by mist, the contours hidden in smoke, Leonardo's *sfumato*. Debbie was standing in the stirrups, holding him. Her hair billowed out from under her pink and red cap, and she seemed as she rode to be centered in him, her balance absolute. I was waiting for her back at the barn. She took off her cap and asked me to hold Bushel's reins. He didn't like it. He started moving toward me, shaking his head and rolling back his lips to exhibit his awful teeth. They were stained various shades of brown from hay, oat husks, bran, and mash and re-minded me of the eroded, unbrushed nubbins dentists showed you when they were trying to coerce you to *floss*. Debbie yanked on the reins. "He's just feeling good," she said. Grooms always said this when their horses were acting rowdy and appeared ready to kick. I remained on guard. Horses always got you when you weren't looking. The other day, Debbie said, she'd been walking down the shedrow, minding her own business, when *clunk,* this new colt of Dick Leavitt's stuck his head out of his stall and wrapped his mouth around her arm. She showed me the purple bruise.

"What'd you do?"

"Went and got a rake and hit him with it."

She squirted liquid soap into a bucket and filled it with water. The solution smelled minty. I led Bushel to a spot near the hotwalker and Debbie started bathing him, working a sponge over his withers. He didn't like this either, not in the chilly fog, and he snorted a few times and backed away. Again Debbie yanked on the reins. "You cut that out," she said, bringing her face close to his, "or I'll go get the shank," a piece of leather rope used for teaching manners. She gave me the sponge and I washed Bushel's right side. It was like washing a car, involving similar motions, sponge to bucket, and sloppy suds, but horse felt better under my hand than chrome had ever done. There was something sensual in the washing, feeling Bushel's bunched muscles and his coat slick with water, and experiencing at the same time the reticulated nature of the backstretch, my eye drawn to other grooms washing other horses all down the shedrow. They seemed to recede into space like the figures reflected in the background bulbs and mirrors of Flemish paintings. Debbie passed me an aluminum sweat scraper, a thin curved blade about a foot long, and I used it to scrape off the excess soap. Then she took Bushel and hooked him to the hotwalker. He felt the pull and began to circle. Midway through the second go-round he let out a whinny, flexed his quarters, and shot both rear legs into the air.

"*Still* feeling good," Debbie said.

I stepped back a few steps, thinking of skulls busted like pumpkins, coils of brains.

Debbie could still remember the day she fell in love with horses. It happened in Virginia when she was a little girl. Her father took her to a horse show and she pressed her nose to the auditorium rail and looked down at the floor of the arena where Morgans and high-stepping Tennessee Walkers were on parade. The pageantry of the event stuck in her mind, and when she was nine she got a pony of her own and won titles all over the state. After graduating a year early from high school, she was offered several jobs but turned them down (the scene was too "political," she says) and instead went to work for a famous trainer of show horses in Massachusetts. She wasn't happy there. The trainer was tough, a stickler for detail. Debbie's day began at six and ended at dusk; she earned next to nothing. In the barn there was a large clock overhead, and every task the grooms had to perform was apportioned by it. Each horse received exactly forty minutes' grooming, then forty minutes' brushing with a currycomb. When the grooms finished, they had to sweep the barn, muck out the stalls, and arrange the dirty straw in a precise checkerboard pattern outside. Debbie lasted about three months. She left after the first frost, slipping away with a friend and boarding a plane for the friend's house in San Rafael, California.

Once she'd settled in Debbie went looking for a job at Bay Meadows. She got some work galloping horses and slowly built up her clientele, handling twelve to thirteen head every morning at three or four dollars a ride. Eventually she left California to work for a man who ran his horses at tracks in the East and Midwest, and made the Grooms' Grand Tour of Major Racing Installations in the United States. Every groom seemed to have made the tour at least once and they returned from it with copious mental notes on the various facilities available—backstretch accommodations, the quality of cafeteria food, the night life nearby. In Delaware Debbie got her trainer's license. The oral exam was difficult, she said, and to illustrate she told me about a man who tried to take it without bothering to study. "What does 'stifle' mean?" the examiners asked him. The man shrugged. "Means I don't get no trainer's license," he said. Debbie was glad she'd made the tour. "Now I know the grass *isn't* greener," she liked to say. She liked working for Glen Nolan. He paid her well and had recently advanced her twenty-five hundred dollars so she could claim an ancient router named Benson, a hard-hitting vet if ever there was one. Benson was stabled at Nolan's farm, burning hay, and rode in by van on days when he was scheduled to race. He was the fourth horse Debbie had owned and she'd made money on all of them. She was shrewd in money matters. Her own wagers, carefully placed, supplemented her income and allowed her to rent a small apartment in El Sobrante. She thought of herself as a homebody who spent quiet evenings among her cats, dogs, books, and friends. Perhaps she needed to make this distinction between her racetrack persona, brisk and efficient, and the more feminine self she was forced to keep hidden. Even though she discouraged them, backstretch Lotharios pursued her avidly. On Saturdays, she worked in pari-mutuels and from its pool of eligible bachelors she drew her suitors. When a young pari-mutuel clerk came by the barn one morning to say hello, dressed to the macho nines in patterned body shirt and aviator glasses, I saw Debbie flustered for the first time, trying to balance herself as she'd done so successfully on Bushel Ruler.

IX

Everybody had a theory about why so many young women came to the track looking for work, but I discarded them in favor of a very simple equation best put by little Liz Taylor in *National Velvet*. "I can't help it, father," Lizzie whined, "I'd rather have that horse happy than go to heaven!" What I saw in the shedrows was an ongoing love affair. For the most part, it revolved around service, and also the aesthetic pleasure to be derived from handling horses, but there was a randy underside to it as well, which could be seen in the smiles of certain ponygirls as they rode off the track after a good gallop, and in the dreamy-eyed look some grooms got as they stroked the flank of a colt. Most women hadn't read D. H. Lawrence, but a few of them raved to me about the books of Walter Farley, which they'd read in adolescence. Farley had written a series of juveniles starring the Black Stallion, who is described as follows when he makes his first appearance on a ships' landing in a small Arabian port:

> White lather ran from the horse's body; his mouth was open, his teeth bared. He was a giant of a horse, glistening black— too big to be pure Arabian. His mane was like a crest, mounting, then falling low. His neck was long and slender, and arched to the small, savagely beautiful head. The head was that of the wildest of all wild creatures—a stallion born wild—and it was beautiful, savage, splendid. A stallion with a wonderful physical perfection that matched his savage, ruthless spirit.

Once a young woman got a job, she was assigned tacitly to one of two prevailing social roles, princess or tramp. Princesses came to work at six in the morning, often with makeup on, lipstick, blusher, even eyeshadow. They were friendly but aloof, smiled but seldom laughed, worked hard, accepted no invitations, and remained untouchable except within the confines of a monogamous relationship. Tramps, it was understood, were fair game. They chewed gum, went braless, liked to party, and screwed around. If a woman slept with a man. once, and only once, in healthy abandon, without any thought of the future, she ran the risk of being consigned forever to trampdom and hit upon by every lackluster dooley in manure-stained jeans.

"That girl who works for so-and-so," said one clucking male groom to another, "I hear she does the trick." Because women were permitted to do "men's work," the backstretch was supposed to be a liberated place, but I saw little evidence of this. More often I felt as if I were back in high school, observing the same tedious sexual constraints.

A few women at Golden Gate seemed suspended momentarily between roles. I saw the slim blonde from the Home Stretch every now and then, wandering around as though shopping for permanence. She'd picked up a friend along the way, a tall girl with pale blue eyes and ice-blond Nordic hair, and together they cruised the backstretch and grandstand waiting for something to happen. There was another woman around whom I thought of as a fallen princess not quite ready to become a tramp. I'd heard that she'd worked once for a trainer, but now she was unemployed. One morning I saw her alone on the infield grass, dressed in a flowing Hawaiian shirt and trousers. While jockeys bundled in rubber suits jogged around her, sweating off pounds, she did handstands and cartwheels, bouncing barefooted off the trunks of palms. Another morning, cold and foggy, she stood next to me during workouts. She wore a watch cap and a navy-blue greatcoat that touched the top of her shoes. Across the shoulders of the coat, thrown there like a fur piece, was a white cat. Every time the cat moved, the fallen princess caught it and returned it to her shoulders. When the sun came out she took off her cap, and long brown hair fell in tangles to her waist.

X

When Pico fell in love he did so with abandon. He became enamored of a grocer's wife in Arezzo who was married to a relative of Lorenzo de' Medici's. Presumably Pico could have carried on an affair, as did so many of his contemporaries, but he wanted all or nothing. So he mounted a night raid, taking along his secretary and twenty other men on horseback, then snatched his mistress from her donjon of commerce and spirited her away to a town nearby, barely escaping with his life. Fifteen men were killed in the skirmish following the kidnap. The siege came to an unhappy conclusion when Pico was arrested. Only Lorenzo's intervention saved him from the gallows. It was impossible for the wife of someone related to the Medici to be unfaithful, he said, and the kidnapped woman was returned to her husband a little the worse for wear. As for Pico, he wasn't capable of concocting such a plan. Certainly his secretary had misled him, said Lorenzo, turning the poor secretary over to the constables.

XI

Bo Twinn was waiting outside the barn when Bill Stallings, the jockey, dismounted and returned Urashima Taro after his morning workout.

"How's the little bastard feeling?" Bo asked.

Stallings handed over the reins. "Real good," he said. He had a Munchkin's voice, sunglasses, puffed cheeks. "Feeling real good."

"Then how come he was pawing in his stall all night keeping me awake?"

"I wouldn't know about that."

"Every time you look," said Bo, addressing nobody in particular, "you find something else wrong. They generally doing something they ain't supposed to when you don't want 'em to be doing it."

"Played softball last night," Stallings announced. "Hurt my damn leg, too."

Bo was unsympathetic. "Go see Headley," he told Stallings. "He'll medicate you."

Pichi was due to run that afternoon and I went in to check on her. She looked anxious. When she saw me coming she backed away, toward the protective recesses of her stall.

"She's *so* radical," Bo said. He was cleaning Urashima's hoofs with a pick, chipping mud and pebbles from under the shoes. "All fillies is finicky this time of year but she's worse. She's a bad doer. If she don't eat, how's she going to run?" He tried to get at Urashima's right front foot but Urashima wouldn't help. Bo slapped him gently below the knee. "C'mon, c'mon, you little bastard, lift it up. You ain't going to no Derby. Did you see this little bastard run?"

Headley's dream horse had finished next to last his first time out. "I saw him."

"Then you know *why* he ain't going. Headley's riding a new boy on Pichi today, that Jimmy Colaneri. He might rate her more kindly. I hope he rates her more kindly."

"How'd you come to work at the track, Bo?"

He gave me an exasperated look, arching his eyebrows. "I was left an orphan is *how*," he said. "In a town outside Houston. My father, he rode jumping horses and us kids knew all about racing. When he died and left me an orphan all I knew to do was to go to a racetrack. Tell me where else a ten-year-old is likely to get a job."

"Which track did you go to?"

"Epsom Downs."

Bo stopped talking abruptly when a man in a pale green shirt materialized in the shedrow doorway and stood there backlit and grinning in a shifty sort of way, as though he'd oiled his lips on getting out of bed.

"Morning," he said.

"Morning yourself."

There was an extended silence during which all the nonhuman sounds of the backstretch seemed to accelerate, the whining of forklifts, goats braying, water sloshing in gutters.

"I was wondering about that filly," the man said. "Appears she's about ready."

"I wouldn't know about that," Bo said. "She's a radical son-of-a-bitch. She might go good or she might not."

The man waited awhile longer, whistling to himself, a low mean tune, and at last touched his hat brim. "Well, all right, then," he said and departed without the information he'd been seeking.

"Damn ten percenters," Bo said bitterly, "they's always looking for something for nothing. That one, he's a jockey agent. I don't like him. He don't work. Why in the hell should I tell him if my horse is fit? If he worked it might be different, 'stead of living off somebody else. Long as a man is working and has a little money, he don't have to take any outstanding wad of shit from anybody. If I don't like something, I just move on. I guess that makes me independent."

He took a red coffee can, dipped it into a bag broken open on the floor, and filled the feed tubs with sweet feed, a mix of rolled oats, rolled corn, barley, and molasses.

"I got my trainer's license, you know. My name's listed in the program."

I'd seen it there, under Headley's name, *Asst. Trainer Elbert A. Twinn*. The designation didn't mean much. Lots of grooms had earned it but few would ever accept the full-time responsibilities inherent in being a trainer.

"Why do they call you Bo?" I asked.

"Comes from Elbert. My brothers and sisters used to call me Elbow and then they shortened it to Bo." He looked around despairingly. "I wonder where the hell Headley is at. He just went home to change clothes but it's almost eleven. Those people, they's supposed to come up and watch Pichi run." He went into his room and made some instant coffee. Two kittens were playing, one hiding under a fringe of blanket and the other, on the bed, pouncing on him. The runt was still around, asleep now on the dresser top near a bottle of after-shave. "I got rid of two so far," Bo said, "but the others, looks like they might be staying."

I respected grooms like Bo, perhaps disproportionately. They lived the most rigorous and honest lives on the backstretch and seemed to have fewer illusions than anybody else. Their lives had an ascetic quality, functioning within a matrix of basic demands, work, food, rest, sex, a little occasional excitement, and peace of mind. Often they were highly principled and uncompromising, which led them to social failure. They were suspicious of owners and trainers alike. On more than one occasion a groom had told me in confidence that he'd left his last employer because he'd been instructed to mistreat the stock. Instead of participating in such malice, imagined or not, grooms moved on, going from trainer to trainer, track to track, state to state, leaving in their wake beer cans and whiskey bottles, broken marriages and promises broken on principle. Sometimes they left for no reason at all, or because the booze or dope had finally fried their circuits. But through it all they remained faithful to some inner model of goodness, an eccentric and singular moral code, and always to the horses.

Bo stomped out his cigarette and kicked the butt under a stall ledge, hiding it. "Those fire inspectors from Berkeley, they come around all the time now. If they'd just fix things up in here nobody'd have to worry." The barns were old and the wood was old and rotting. "I saw a bad fire at Exhibition Park," Bo said.

"Some crazy guy, he was mad at somebody, he lit the straw on fire with gasoline. The horses went crazy. I could hear them a long way off. My boss saw them burning up and he had a heart attack on the spot. Just dropped dead. I left eight days later."

It was getting warm in the barn and I thought of summer. "You going to work the county fairs, Bo?"

"I don't work no fairs."

"What'll you do?"

"Either go down to Hollywood Park or take a vacation."

"What do you do on vacation?"

He smirked. "Little as possible."

He went to his room and shaved and changed clothes, and when he came back he looked ready for a night on the town in Cheyenne, Wyoming. I was going to kid him about it, but he was getting more and more anxious. Headley was still missing and if he didn't show up soon Bo would have to deal with the Sandomirs.

"Probably I'll go south," he said, sitting down in a lawn chair. "I got a three-quarter-ton pickup out back I just finished rebuilding. I can go anywhere I want. I might even go to Texas."

"Texas?"

"Hell, yes, *Texas*. They got racing there. I know people around. There's lots of guys that know me. I still got family down there, too. I'd like to see them."

"You ever try any other kind of work?"

"I thought about it once," he said, "when I got out of the service back east, but I ended up at Narragansett. The track froze solid, that's how cold it was that winter. I don't know," he said, collecting Pichi's tack, the bridle and bit, "I guess this is really all I *know* to do."

Headley arrived at last, and he met the Sandomirs and escorted them to the paddock. They stood together on the elevated rectangle fenced in wrought iron and called the Owners' Pavilion, watching the horses stride onto the track, where each in turn was claimed by an outrider on a pony, the movement as sinuous as the stitchery on the brocade of a Sienese madonna. Pichi was even calmer this time and went off at twenty-three to one. Colaneri handled her well against a cheaper field and she finished a good if somewhat unbelievable third. The race went in 1:12 flat, about average for a maiden sprint, and it became possible to entertain the idea that Pichi might someday win. Headley was gloating. "Did you see those people?" he asked. "They acted like the horse won the Kentucky Derby." The Sandomirs *were* very pleased. Mary was hugging anybody she could get her hands on, and would've hugged Bo, too, but he was out on the track helping Colaneri down from the saddle and retrieving Pichi.

XII

When I watched Bo working I thought of the young men who were apprenticed to Florentine painters and sculptors during the Renaissance. They too kept manic schedules, working from five in the morning until eight at night, sweeping clean the studio floors, tossing garbage into the street, fetching bread and cheese, grinding colors and mixing pigments, priming wood panels with an undercoat of ashes made from chicken bones, a charcoal base for permeable *gesso*, doing a hundred such menial tasks so that Pollaiuolo or Verrocchio or some other master could step up, brush in hand, and apply the final strokes unencumbered, just as Headley, on arriving at the barn, found waiting for him a horse as blemish-free and fine-tuned as possible.

Like Bo, most apprentices never went beyond the rank of assistant trainer. They lived out their lives transferring the master's cartoons to chapel walls and filling in background areas, blue skies too simple for the master to bother with, but there was still something noble about their service. In the case of grooms, this nobility came from husbanding the stock. The job was pure in its way, untainted, and its dimensions had never been expressed so beautifully as in a groom's handbook published in the nineteenth century, *A Treatise on the Care, Treatment and Training of the English Racehorse,* by Richard Darvill, late of the Seventh Hussars. Darvill was a perfectionist and carried his devotion to extremes. Horses should be given only water from rivers, he said, or rainwater, and stable boys, those lowly groom-aspirants, should harvest the green feed (tares, vetches, lucerne, and clover) from the pasture on the hour so it stayed cool and fresh. The plants "should be cut before they begin to blossom, when they are young," wrote Darvill, "and full of juice."

XIII

From my grandstand seat I looked down at the paddock and there was Debbie Thomas leading Bushel Ruler around, both of them groomed and promising, her blond hair setting off the dark rippling of his coat. This was Bushel's debut. He looked strong and full of purpose, and Debbie had told me he was ready to win. At any moment I expected to feel the sensation that always accompanied the magic. I experienced it most vividly in my body, where I felt a sudden slackening of tensions, and then a lightness all over, as though I'd just lost twenty pounds. When I was in this state I never doubted that my horse would win. Sometimes the race itself seemed anticlimactic. Nothing was happening, though, nothing at all. I tried to remember how it had felt to wash Bushel, the water and soap, the feel of his muscles, but the details remained fixed in their arc, useless to me now. In spite of my doubts I bet the horse as heavily as I'd ever bet any horse, knowing even as I laid my money down that I was in violation of some important principle.

I had ten long minutes to wait, and the couple sitting in front of me were making things worse with their constant chatter. They were from Cleveland, visiting an Albany relative, a bald old coot with a flame-red crown, and they kept talking about the Boy Mayor. "Kucinich's honest as all get out," the Cleveland man would say, "he just won't do what the crooks tell him to do." The Cleveland lady would respond by rolling up the sleeves of her dress a little higher and pitching in *her* two cents. "It's not just because he's Polish we like him," she'd say, "he means to do right by everybody, even the coloreds." I was perversely fascinated by the conversation, which went on and on, disrupting handicappers left and right, but at the same time I wished I had a manual of racetrack etiquette to present to these visitors from Ohio, one with as much bite as Giovanni della Casa's. "When you have blown your nose," della Casa advised his ill-mannered Florentine compatriots, "you should not open your handkerchief and inspect it, as if pearls or rubies had dropped out of your skull."

"Who do you like in this race, Ralph?" the coot asked his guest.

Before he could answer his wife extracted two dollars from her purse and waved them around.

"I don't care who *he* likes," she said, "you go bet that pretty number-two horse for me. That Bushel Whatzisname."

This cut me to the quick. I hated to be in line at a window and hear the person in front of me play the horse I intended to play.

Such occurrences hurt my chances, stuffing too many expectations under a single saddle, and the Cleveland woman's commitment would be even worse, weightier, more fraught with neurosis. She was gross, she was stupid, she loved the Boy Mayor, and I knew I was sunk. Before my eyes the city of Adocentyn rose in reprimand. Dogs barked, lions roared, bulls lowered their heads and rammed into the walls, and from the eastern gate eagles took flight, their talons festooned with losing tickets. The magic could not be forced. It was instead a matter of being receptive, of sitting still, of recognizing the moment and then seizing it as Pico had seized his inamorata.

I had a few seconds' worth of elation when Bushel broke well and moved into second place, and I got another jolt when he was still second on the turn, and my heart was beating but good when he was *still* second going into the stretch, but then he began to fade, shortening his stride and sinking back into the commonplace, his ears drooping, his tail sagging, his body unable to sustain the effort just as I'd been unable to sustain the illusion. Together we watched as the other horses disappeared into the distance, dust in our eyes, space stretching out before us, and Sunday's Best, neat as a new suit, spitclean as a barbered head, receding from sight, galloping through the pinhole of victory.

I stopped at Nolan's barn to see Debbie, but she was talking to Gardell, the trainer, and neither of them looked ready for company. Debbie's cheeks were flushed and she was collecting tack with a fury. Bushel was already on the hotwalker. Some people say that horses know when they've lost, but I didn't notice any change in him. Maybe it would show next race, when he had less pride on which to draw. For now he was just circling. The next morning I learned why Debbie had seemed so angry. Bushel had been claimed by Mel Eisen, who trained for Dallas Black. Apparently Eisen had been tipped off to Bushel's potential when he saw him in a training race, running well against much more expensive stock. Debbie was disconsolate. She told me she'd cried for two straight hours after the race. Later that night, though she wasn't supposed to, she'd snuck over to Eisen's barn to check on Oli. When he saw her coming, he stuck his head out of his stall and whinnied and nickered, just as he'd always done in the past.

XIV

I watched the Kentucky Derby in the press box. The race was a pure and emotional thing, and it brought us back to the essence of the sport and bleached our bones of caring. I came away from it feeling refreshed, and I thought how nice it would be actually to go to Kentucky someday and watch the race from that crackerjack grandstand and drink overpriced mint juleps and smell the ripe perfume of southern girls. This was the start of something, hope.

That night I went on a minor-league celebration with Arnold Walker, who'd finished the day ahead and couldn't tolerate all that extra cash in his pockets. We had a big dinner at Spenger's and Arnold spilled some cabernet on his good gray vest. Next he dragged me into the room where they have the oyster bar and wall-size TV. "It's not so bad," he said. "Here, have a seat. I think you'll like it." He forced me to drink another bottle of wine and watch a beauty pageant. The semifinalists walked onstage through an arch formed by the crossed sabers of some cadets from the Citadel while the Citadel choir sang "You Light Up My Life." "I love it," Arnold said. "I absolutely love it." The Question Period followed the parade. Leroy Neiman, the Famous Artist, was a judge and he tried to trick one of the girls into revealing something out of the ordinary. "If you could pick one woman," Leroy said, winding up, ready to toss a spitball, *"other than your mother,* as your model, who would it be and why?" Miss Massachusetts thought it over. "My grandmother," she said. Miss Florida told what a bad driver she was, having accidents all the time and once driving right onto a porch where some old lady was eating breakfast. "I'll bet she takes drugs," said Arnold. "What'll you give me?" I wouldn't give him anything. We watched the coronation and the tears and then I went back to the Terrace and fell asleep in my clothes. When I woke in the morning the first thing I saw was the globe Ted had given me. I spun it around, looking for Italy.

Chapter Six

In a notebook I had written *"Firenze:* Florence, flowers, efflorescence," but this was far too romantic, only part of the truth.

II

In 1963 I kept several secret notebooks, recording observations, deep thoughts, ideas for poems and novels never to be written. I was nineteen and was supposed to be planning my future, but with the war in Vietnam escalating it seemed to me that I had no future, not of the sort my background and education proposed. College had also been a disappointment. In my first two years I'd learned the meaning of J. Press, how to look as though I'd gone to Exeter, how to make fish-house punch, the quickest route to Skidmore, and a little about art and literature. This was not what I had expected. An abiding disillusionment set in and I flunked American Ideals and Institutions, a required course, and drove my Chevrolet Impala across the frozen lawns of neighboring fraternities, destroying snow sculptures in the process. When the snow melted I went with friends to a boathouse by a lake and drank beer all night long. At dawn somebody almost shot me through the head with his .22. You could say I was confused. I accepted strange invitations, found myself in taverns in towns with one stoplight, existed on pickled eggs and whatever else pitying ladies happened to feed me, and once woke up on a couch in a minister's study somewhere near the Canadian border. Not good, I thought, not good at all. A friend came to the rescue by telling me about a study program offered by another university, a semester abroad in Florence. "It's cheap and they'll take almost anybody," he said. Certainly I fit the bill.

III

We left on a cruise ship, American Export Lines. Somebody brought around champagne on a tray and several passengers operating under the influence of B-movies smashed their glasses on the deck, much to the stewards' consternation. The man next to me wept softly into his handkerchief and kept waving long after the New York skyline had dropped from view. I felt no sadness myself, only exhilaration. It never occurred to me that the people back at the dock might not be there when I returned. They had a fixity of purpose in my mind, a rooted quality that in part I was escaping. For a long time there was nothing to see except birds and water. The water changed colors constantly and sometimes rolled forward in a spume-dappled band of aquamarine, but after a week or so I got tired of looking at it and went into the bar. The bartender had a funny little goatee and thought I was a rogue, young and wild and flirting with danger. Apparently the sea infected everybody with romantic notions, even hard-bitten guys from the Bronx. I sat by a window and watched the old couples taking constitutionals and the children chasing after quoits and Ping-Pong balls. It seemed odd that they were determined to perpetuate the most mundane aspects of existence when there were porpoises on the horizon and the liberating dreams of Ishmael to be dreamed.

Tangier was our first port of call. On shore, bells were ringing and traders gathered in the dust to hawk knives, hassocks, opium, fake Swiss watches, girls, boys, kif, fezzes, parrots, and tours of the Arab quarter. I ate some obligatory couscous in a dank and therefore authentic restaurant and spent hours standing on the huge granite blocks along the Mediterranean littoral, watching gulls, ships, and fishermen. I think I wrote some verses about the sea. It was difficult to accept the validity of a foreign country when you knew that at a predestined hour you had to leave it, probably forever. Tangier might cease to exist or perhaps shuffle its elements into a more sophisticated diorama for the next bunch of tourists.

In Lisbon we had a little more time. I saw the famous mustachioed ladies with baskets on their heads and took a taxi to Estoril, reputed playground of the world's leading deposed monarchs. The monarchs sat beneath striped beach umbrellas, wearing sunglasses and knit bathing suits with the waistbands pulled up almost to their pectorals. They were fat and jolly and loved to splash in the sea, accompanied by thin bronzed women in bikinis. They made exile look attractive. I remember drinking a gin and tonic on the terrace of some café and feeling very cosmopolitan, as though the collar of my shirt didn't really button down.

We debarked in Genoa and went by bus to Florence. The school was located right across from a small piazza presided over by a statue of Girolamo Savonarola, the Dominican monk whose apocalyptic fervor had dulled the spirit of the Renaissance. All the students were to live with local families; an old woman in a shiny black dress stepped forward to claim me. Her hands were leathery and her cheeks were glossed with broken capillaries. The administrator called her *marchesa* but either the title was honorary or she'd been deposed like the monarchs, because her flat was dark, musty, cold, and impoverished. She shared it with her son and his wife and their son Paolo, who was thirteen. For dinner the marchesa served soup, boiled beef, and fennel but no wine, not a drop of it, and we had a circumscribed conversation about New York and spaghetti.

"You are from New York?"

"*Sì. Mi piace questo* . . . soup."

"You like soup then?"

"*Sì.* Very good."

"*Grazie.* Tomorrow I give you spaghetti. You like it?"

"*Sì.* I like it very much."

"Do they eat it in New York?"

"*Sì.* They eat it."

"*Buono,*" the marchesa said, tossing her napkin on the table, "*domani spaghetti.*"

After supper I went to my room and a few minutes later Paolo showed up, wearing a baseball cap and carrying a new mitt, which smelled of the olive oil he'd rubbed into the pocket. He played shortstop for the Firenze Lions, a group of adolescent soccer refugees, and he wanted to hear all about the Yankees. I told him what I could, in sign language and gestures, and he suggested we play catch in the hallway. It was so dark I had trouble seeing the ball. It kept bouncing off my chest. Next Paolo brought out a baseball board game his uncle in Chicago had sent him and we played it until midnight. He beat me badly. "Someday I'm going to America," he said, signing off, and finally I got into bed. The mattress was soft, though, and I couldn't sleep. The image of Paolo with his cap and mitt haunted me. I had the feeling that wherever I traveled, Luxembourg, the Seychelles islands, some native would take my hand

and lead me into a dark hallway and ask me to play catch. This seemed an unavoidable circumstance, an aspect of my birthright.

IV

The Florence I chose to live in wasn't an actual city but instead the legendary Florence of Lorenzo the Magnificent. His face was the map of the territory, fleshy, broad, shrewd, a little flushed from drink, and his pursuits, I imagined, were mine: art, women, wine, and poetry. I never thought about villainy or political machinations or conspirators like the Pazzi family, who'd been hung from gibbets outside the Medici palace. I wanted to forget about such things, even as I was forgetting for the moment about home. My favorite hangout was the Piazza Signoria very early in the morning, before the tourists had arrived, when the museums and sidewalk cafés were still closed and waiters were just taking the chairs down from tables and sweeping up cigarette butts with long-handled push brooms. They looked half-asleep, their hair uncombed and their chins unshaven. They seemed to move in slow motion, unhurried. I thought this had to do with the statues along the Loggia dei Lanzi, with the copy of Michelangelo's David in front of the Palazzo Vecchio. The elegantly carved marble on view extended into a historical vastness and seemed to imply that Florence had once been peopled by giants, beings of such magnitude and roundness that the waiters were only echoes, soft discordant notes played upon a vaguely recollected scale. So the waiters moved slowly, without struggling under the weight of expectations, and I relaxed on the Loggia next to Cellini's statue of Perseus, letting the morning go.

When the Uffizi opened I went in and moved through its galleries as through blocks of time, down long sunlit corridors hung with tapestries, watching the black-robed priests, visitors from Padua, from Genoa or Livorno, as they tracked Christ's image around the museum. With a half-liter of chianti under my belt I could follow the course of the river flowing behind Piero della Francesca's portrait of the Duke of Urbino to its logical terminus in some perfect valley beyond the frame, or be stood on my head by the lances, horses, hounds, and hares colliding in Uccello's "Battle of San Romano." *Uccello,* a nickname, *the bird,* was really Paolo di Dono, a gentle soul who loved animals and passed interminable hours reducing the world to a series of shaped and interlocking planes, earth-toned but broken on occasion by the brilliance of horses—white, rust, gray, silver—and crimson lances piercing the sky. *Quit studying perspective and come to bed,* his wife shouted, but Uccello remained faithful to the geometry of his flying forms. Piero di Cosimo was more eccentric still and painted nymph- and satyr-ridden landscapes from which suffering was excluded. He hated priests and doctors and loved instead wild savage things, essential Nature. The isolative drumming of a good hard rain pleased him greatly, although he disliked lightning with its hint of technological futures. His cottage was overgrown with fruit trees and vines, which he wouldn't prune, and these unruly tendrils seemed to reach across centuries and touch me there in the Uffizi. All the linked canvases were a stream and moved like blood through the building, through the stones of the city, and when I stepped outside at last the streets and domes were bathed in gold, and bells were ringing everywhere, signifying dusk.

V

Naturally I fell in love, first with a short dark-haired girl who wanted no part of me and then with a pretty girl from Tennessee with highlights in her hair. She loved books and music and tolerated the bad verses (some about the sea) of would-be poets. We rode bicycles through Cascine Park and bought watermelon slices from vendors and later, when the weather turned cold, chestnuts in newspaper cones. This seemed remarkable to us, the shift of seasons echoed in commerce, autumn ripeness giving way to gloves, embers, and bursting shells. After our relationship was firmly established Suzanne presented me with the address of one of the few places in town serving draft beer. It was called *Tredici Gobbi,* Thirteen Hunchbacks, and we went there often at my request. One night I chained my bicycle to a window somewhere and never found it again. Love is dangerous, I thought, but Florence pushed its lovers to extremes. There was Pico, of course, and also that excessive lyric of Lorenzo's that compared his mistress's pale beauty to the soft white fat around a kidney.

At midterm Suzanne and I hitchhiked to Rome, which was a great adventure, the first time I'd stayed in a hotel room with a girl. I tried to be orderly, to pick up my socks and underwear, but after a day or two I saw that intimacy, for all its revelations, was more natural than the politely enforced distances of society. Rome was more metropolitan than Florence, more forward-looking and contentious. Modern apartment buildings were threatening useless antiquities like the Coliseum. On the Via Veneto fashionable types studied themselves in plate-glass windows, and we kept expecting to see Mastroianni or Fellini sitting at one or another of the cafés. Michelangelo still dominated the old city, but for the preening *ragazzi* of the boulevards, Cinecittá supplied the necessary icons. We tried to see the frescoes at the Sistine Chapel but without scaffolding it was almost impossible. The heavenly continent was vast, but dulled by poor lighting. It amazed us to see people eating bananas and salami sandwiches while walking around the chapel floor searching for Adam. In a biergarten one night we met a German who told us they set up bleachers in there whenever the Pope made an appearance, but we didn't believe him. He was from the Protestant lowlands and surely antipathetic to the Church. At night we crawled into bed, warm beneath the coverlets, and listened to whores bargaining with their clients on the Spanish Steps.

Things turned sour on the return trip when a crazy man picked us up. He was pig-fat, with an ascot stuffed into his shirt and kidskin driving gloves on his piggy fingers. When we stopped for lunch at a roadside *trattoria,* he called for the manager and asked if the doorknob, a heavy but unspectacular bronze item, was for sale. The manager shrugged in the provincial manner, unscrewed plating and knob and accepted a few thousand *lire.* Outside the crazy man laughed hysterically. "A real bargain," he said, wiping his eyes. He stopped next at an ancient fortified town on a hillside and told us to look around while he did some business at a local hotel. We waited an hour and then I went to check on him. "He's taking a nap," said the desk clerk. Two shady ladies in mesh stockings and tiny skirts sat at a bar adjacent to the lobby, ready to take naps with other adventurers. We tried to hitch another ride, but the town was so medieval that not a single car passed through the square.

Finally the crazy man emerged. He was apologetic and I thought maybe his performance was over, but twenty miles from Florence, just at nightfall, he lifted the flap of his sportcoat and said, "Look at this." He had a leather sheath attached to his belt. A hunting knife was in it. Minutes later he turned off the highway and onto an unmarked dirt road which led to the lights of another hillside town. He was whistling some popular song between his teeth and I still remember its annoying pitch. The road was bad and he had to drive slowly, and I thought if I slugged him on the next curve and grabbed the wheel I could ram us into the hillside without killing us at the same time. But then the crazy man spoke again.

"There's a nice hotel ahead," he said. "We'll spend the night there."

"We have to get back to Florence," I said, "Maybe you'd better let us out."

And here I expected the knife to come flashing out of its sheath to press against my neck, but the crazy man, being crazy, just braked to a halt.

"Too bad you don't like me," he said, reaching across to push open my door.

When he drove away, I could hear the doorknob rattling in his trunk. We hiked three cold miles through stunning darkness, back to the highway, and when a family in a little Peugeot picked us up and gave us cigarettes and heat, I felt as if we'd been saved from drowning, snatched from the edges of the sea.

VI

One afternoon I stopped at the Piazza San Marco and toured the cloister. In a rear corridor I came upon Savonarola's cell, cold and sparely furnished, and saw the portrait of him painted by Fra Bartolommeo. It had a chilling effect. His face, shown in hooded profile, was almost white, as though dusted with powder, and his cheeks were sunken and his powerful black eyes were set back in bony hollows. He looked cadaverous, the antithesis of Lorenzo. I remembered the omens that had supposedly preceded the Magnificent's demise: a hurricane, a lion devoured by other lions in a den at the Signoria, a Medici escutcheon blown free of the roof and shattered on the left side of the palace, *a la sinistra,* the sinister side, and the story told in some quarters of a fire-breathing ox seen chasing a woman through the streets. Lorenzo's doctor gave him a solution sprinkled with powdered diamonds, the prescribed remedy for a financier, but he died anyway. Savonarola visited him on his deathbed; two years later the city was caught up in moral fervor.

VII

My friend Nelson lived in a rundown villa in Fiesole, the Etruscan hill town from which the original settlers had descended to build Florence. I used to visit him there in his dukedom of olive trees, vineyards, relics, chapels, broken cisterns, lizards, and crumbling stones. Fiesole was a magical place, the ancient outpost of sorcerers. In the evenings, wearing ethereal costumes and masks, they crept from their grottoes to draw water, and on some nights you could still feel their presence, a sudden chill when the light shifted and the city below fell to darkness. Nelson's marchesa, who resembled Sophia Loren in miniature, drove off this chill by putting another log on the fire and serving some rum. Before dinner she would call to her children. The eldest, Eduardo, a Communist studying at the university, came readily to the table, and so did the middle son, Tommaso, a ravaged kid who'd starved himself down to ninety pounds to avoid conscription into the Italian Army, but often we had to go looking for the third child, Giorgio. He was a sweet boy whose brain was tuned to inaudible sounds and he got lost in the ruins, chasing birds or mice or shadows. After the meal Tommaso played his guitar and sang folk songs, or Eduardo lectured us on the political realities of contemporary Europe, but Giorgio never said anything at all. He just stared at his plate and scratched his head, which made the hair stand up in black bunches. Tommaso took a weekend trip with us once to Viareggio on the Ligurian coast north of Pisa, and he was astonished to see what Americans were willing to pay for food and rooms. The hotel seemed inexpensive to us, especially at sunset when we could stand on a balcony and look out at the Apuan Alps. Pale declivities were revealed within the folds, coloring pink and rose and even red. Tommaso told us these were quarries, exposed veins of marble. The village of Carrara was nearby and the great blocks chipped from the mountains were destined to end up there, just as they had done in the days of Michelangelo.

VIII

Around Thanksgiving, Paolo insisted on taking me to the Firenze Lions' ballfield and giving me a workout. It was a tufted square on the outskirts of the city with an old screen backstop and a nearby church for slumping batters to pray in. All the Lions, ten or twelve of them, congregated in centerfield and I hit them fungoes, towering fly balls that impressed them mightily. They were only children, of course, and none of them had ever seen a Major Leaguer play. Afterward they crowded around me just the way sandlot kids used to crowd around the Babe when he paid a visit to Baltimore. Their adulation made me uneasy, though; I wanted to be celebrated for my aspirations, not my skill with a bat.

On the bus back to the city, Paolo asked me if I'd send him a Yankees cap when I got home.

"I'm not going home, Paolo," I said.

IX

School let out just before Christmas; by mid-December I was in a panic. Another ocean crossing loomed ahead, the motion this time unmistakably retrograde. I told friends I was going to stay behind, rent a room in a cheap *pensione,* write a novel, and live, if necessary, off crusts scavenged from tourists' plates, but I didn't have the courage. Instead, after final exams, like everyone else, I started packing, filling my suitcase with souvenirs, photos, postcards of the Duomo and the Gates of Paradise. For my mother I bought a portfolio of art prints, *Maestri dei Colori,* but this proved to be another error in judgment. When she tore off the cellophane wrapper, the prints inside were bright and out of register, untrue to the originals.

Chapter Seven

But my experience in Florence renewed me in many ways and for years after I took sustenance from what had happened to me there. In bad or difficult times I would retreat briefly into memory and think about the Uffizi or evenings spent on the roof of the British Council Library reading Yeats, who was my favorite poet then, and looking across the alley to an apartment window in which an old woman sat framed before her sewing machine, patching together fragments of cloth. She was always there in the evening, whenever I was there, and in my mind she became associated with the cathedrals' ringing-out at dusk. "Then bells," I would write in a bad Yeatsian imitation, "and a familiar machine."

So far at Golden Gate I'd felt nothing comparable to that Florentine release. The sadness was still with me, although for hours at a time my attention to the races did manage to obliterate all other concerns. Originally I thought this would be enough, nine shots of adrenaline every afternoon bracketed by the deep concentration necessary for handicapping, but I was learning too much about how the track worked, which took the shine off my enthusiasm. Betting was indeed a shock to the system, but it was the most obvious hit, the surface stuff. I still believed something special was going on at the track, at any track, but I was starting to suspect it had more to do with nesting birds than with money, speed, or class.

Still it was impossible not to be hopeful with spring firmly established at last. Even the stoopers who scoured the grandstand in search of carelessly discarded winning tickets were in bloom. They'd put away their winter clothes, fedoras, furs, and oversize topcoats, and were resplendent now in detoxified Salvation Army windbreakers and new sneakers *with* laces. On the backstretch everybody was talking baseball, the ascent of the Giants, the descent of the A's; and then one evening, in absolute vernal confirmation, I saw two jockeys playing catch on the infield grass. They reminded me of Firenze Lions, emblems of cross-pollination.

II

Soon the jockeys were joined by other jockeys and valets still in their track-issue uniforms, white shirts and dark green trousers, and grooms and a few trainers and an agent or two and a couple of girls in pigtails and argyle socks. Dale Steward, the ultimate cowboy trainer, hit fungoes in the general direction of the barns while somebody else arranged shirt and sweater bases to form a diamond. The jockeys took the field. Art Lobato pitched for them, and Richie Galarsa, who'd ridden seven mounts that afternoon, played second base. Both were in terrific shape. Galarsa, nineteen, stood about five feet one and rode at a hundred and eight pounds, and you'd need a scalpel to find any fat on him. His shoulders were very broad, like those of a weight lifter, and his arms were thickly knotted with muscles.

His torso tapered down in a classic V to a flat stomach and narrow boyish hips, composing the sort of physique advertised in strength-and-health publications.

But Galarsa didn't have to exercise, riding kept him fit. His legs were his greatest asset. Like all jockeys he rode not so much sitting as standing, hunched forward in a crouch with his boots hooked into the stirrups and his buttocks poised a few inches above the tiny saddle. If he let himself go or missed a few days owing to an injury or suspension, an afternoon's work could reduce his upper thighs to mush. Jockeys' knees often buckled or developed calcium deposits, and cartilage and tendon problems were commonplace. Riding when you were tired was another danger. Then you got careless and your legs gave slightly and your feet slipped suddenly from the stirrups. This was called losing the irons, and it was the most immediately painful experience a rider could have, for it brought him down testicles-first on his mount's spine.

For most jockeys the day had begun a little before dawn. They were out at the track by six to gallop horses for trainers, in hopes of getting a riding assignment in the afternoon, when it counted. Even stars like Tony Diaz, who didn't have to hustle any more, participated in the ritual. Diaz was the only million-dollar jock at Golden Gate, with purses totaling $1,380,172 in 1977, and he was the most stylish dude I'd ever seen on horseback. One morning I watched him take a beautiful bay mare five furlongs over the turf course. He wore a black silk shirt, camel-colored trousers creased like paper, and boots polished so bright they sparkled in the sun. All the while he was riding he kept a lit cigarette between his lips, dragging on it nonchalantly. When he dismounted he took off the hard protective liner he had on his head and replaced it with a big Stetson with a brim like wings. The hat functioned both as a joke and a sign of class. Diaz was cool, he was having fun. When workouts ended he could go home and rest easy until post time, his future secure.

Less fortunate jockeys retired to the Jockeys' Room, a purgatorial two-story building near the grandstand, where they waited out the afternoon. The room was a monument to slaughtered minutes, and the clutter inside was astounding. On the lower floor, lockers were crammed in one against another, spilling talc, tape, socks, clothing, deodorant, cologne, wallets, and pinups. Benches and folding chairs were set at varying angles and formed a labyrinth in which at least one half-naked jockey seemed always to be trapped. Sometimes friends shouted helpful instructions to the trapped man, but their voices were lost in the jumble of sound coming from TV sets and radios, which played competitively, pitting *Days of Our Lives* against Golden Oldies. Reception was always bad, fuzzed by hair driers and electric razors. Jockeys loved to look good and were willing to put in the time required to sculpt a perfect pompadour or wave. They liked fancy shirts and bell-bottomed jeans, which gave their legs a longer line, but they had trouble keeping clothes in press, because of all the steam in the air. It billowed out in misty clouds from the steam room and left a dapple of moisture on the skin. You could see it on the upper lips of tall out-of-place agents, and on the noses of the tack salesmen who stumbled around showing off their wares, slick new whips and boots, enough leather for a dozen sadomasochists.

In the midst of the hubbub, valets went about their business. They took care of jockeys' gear, shining boots and collecting silks and making sure things were in order, for which they earned a small salary plus tips. A few of them had once been jockeys, but the lesson this might have taught current performers went largely unlearned. Riders had king-size egos. Bickering among them was constant, and fistfights occurred so frequently that a ranking of contenders could be compiled. Jorge Aragon would head the list. He'd been set down, or suspended, so many times that backstretch wags suggested he quit riding and become a bantamweight. Aragon paid no attention. His English was bad and besides, the jokes weren't funny. Every suspension cost him money. And once he climbed onto a horse's back he seemed out of control, wild and reckless, and he kept making passionate errors. Recently during a race he'd stolen another boy's whip after he'd dropped his own, reaching across the pack to snatch it away, and had of course been set down again by the stewards. The fans loved him for taking chances, but Aragon's face was often long and his demeanor sad and mopey.

Upstairs, jocks with stable metabolism could buy a burger or BLT at a grill spackled with grease, or sunbathe on a terrace overlooking the backstretch, or shoot pool or play cards or bet among themselves on when the first Chinaman in sneakers would walk through the south admissions gate. Gambling was not encouraged, but jockeys wagered valorously on anything from pinochle to exactas. They were accustomed to an accelerated lifestyle and it took a certain amount of hard cold cash to maintain it. Riding races was sometimes not enough. The fee for handling a losing mount ranged from thirty to thirty-five dollars, and when you considered that many jockeys rode less than once a day, and almost never on a winner, it wasn't difficult to ascertain that the elaborate new Firebirds and Toronados in the jockeys' parking lot were the result of supplemental income. Not even the lowliest bugboy drove a battered Volkswagen like those cruising the obstructed streets of Berkeley.

The busier jockeys with a few mounts on the afternoon's card kept to themselves and studied the *Form*. They tried to devise a strategy for each race they were to ride in, checking out the competition, looking to see what was on either side of them, early speed or closing foot, but this was mostly an intellectual exercise because races seldom turned out as anticipated. Even when the break went right, with all the horses where they ought to be, you could count on an apprentice or some other inexperienced rider to foul things up. They bumped you or shut you off or drove recklessly toward holes that didn't exist, and sometimes you ended up just trying to stay alive instead of winning. This was especially true at cheaper tracks where unskilled riders flourished. Nobody liked to talk about it, but riding racehorses was the most dangerous sport around. On muddy days, you couldn't see despite wearing six pairs of goggles, flipping one spattered pair after another onto your cap, and then, too, there were accidents, sore animals breaking a leg and falling down right in the middle of the pack. Older jockeys said this happened more often now than it used to, and they were careful in selecting which stock they'd ride. Bad spills, busted limbs, concussions, teeth forced free of gums, hemorrhoids, these were all occupational hazards, and so was dying. Just after Tanforan opened, Robert Pineda, twenty-four, fell from his horse and was trampled to death at Pimlico. Pineda's brother Alvaro had died three years earlier at Santa Anita, when his mount reared in the starting gate and crushed his skull.

Such events had to be forgotten as quickly as possible. Death-obsessed riders were worthless on the track. Their defensive style stood out in bold relief against the style of young riders like Galarsa, who learned fast and were strong enough to hold faltering horses together in the stretch. This was a much-valued talent, a gift like ESP or perfect pitch, second only to the greatest gift of all, the Gift of Hands. Jockeys talked to their mounts with their hands, with their palms and fingers, but only a few rare individuals had flesh fine enough to relay messages in an uninterrupted flow. Everybody admired Laffit Pincay, who was strong, with big arms and a massive back, and could bully horses into submission (he was especially good with stallions), making them do what he wanted them to do, but his hands were nothing when compared to Bill Shoemaker's. The Shoe was a genius, an uncanny sensory package, even though he rode less forcefully than he used to. He just sat on a filly, touched her lightly on the neck, made a mooching sound in her ear, and then guided her gently home without ever going to his whip. He'd won nearly a quarter of the thirty-one thousand races he'd ridden in, and nobody could explain his success except by referring to his hands. They were tiny and held in as much esteem as those in the famous Dürer drawing. Not a few people on the backstretch would demand an autopsy when the Shoe's soul ascended at last into heaven.

Out on the infield the jockeys were enjoying themselves. Even the most careworn faces were listing toward innocence. The girl in argyle kneesocks made a fancy catch and blushingly accepted her teammates' cheers. When she ran in after the third out a few players cheered her in more subtle fashion, hugging her in the appropriate places and whispering what were no doubt batting instructions in her ear. The jockeys held the lead going into the fifth inning, but then their opponents made a move. With runners on second and third, Dale Steward was summoned to the plate to pinch-hit. Steward kicked off his boots, took off his hat, spat out the grass blade between his teeth, and rubbed dirt into his palms. He wanted badly to succeed. He took a wild cut at Lobato's first pitch and missed it by a mile. "Shee-it," he said softly, stepping away and shaking his head as though he'd never missed a pitch before. He hit Lobato's next delivery on a line over the center fielder's head. The ball kept climbing toward the *campanile* on the distant Berkeley campus, and Steward watched it fly, his eyes wide as a ten-year-old's and his stockinged feet gliding over the grass.

III

The soul, said Plato, was like a chariot being pulled in two different directions. One horse, the nag of the senses, drew it down toward earth, while a second horse, who loved goodness, struggled to carry it upward toward God. Only a strong driver could control the horses and keep them in harmony, Charioteer Reason. Matteo Palmieri, a Florentine businessman, had a different opinion. In his long poem, "The City of Life," he said that souls were angels who'd refused to take sides during Satan's rebellion. For this offense God had exiled them into human flesh, ordering them to choose now between good and evil. Machiavelli seemed unconcerned about the soul's progress. "The worst that can happen to you is to die and go to Hell," said a character in his *Mandragola.* "But such multitudes have died before you, and in Hell there are so many nice people."

IV

Bill Mahorney was on the terrace of the Jockeys' Room working on his tan. He wore a brown bathing suit and his skin was almost the same color. His hair had a sunbleached blondish tint, like surfers' hair, and at thirty-six he combed it carefully to hide the bald spots underneath. Mahorney liked the heat. When the weather was cold, arthritis stiffened him up and he could feel the plastic and steel in his body. Nearby, some younger jockeys wearing white nylon riding pants cut off at the knees like jeans were leaning over the terrace ledge and watching pretty girls come strolling through the gates, but Mahorney kept his distance.

He was a loner, professional, arrogant, with a tendency to analyze things too deeply. This had gotten him into trouble in the past. Too much thinking was the enemy of instinct, and without instinct riders were nothing. But because he was so good Mahorney had survived.

Currently he was third in the jockey standings at Golden Gate, with over forty wins, but he handled almost as many stakes winners as Tony Diaz. As a contract rider for Chuck Murphy's stable he rode all Murphy's horses, and there were some nice animals, particularly two-year-olds, in the bunch. He rode for other trainers, too, almost always on horses with a chance to win, five or six times a day. Most jockeys envied him, but for Mahorney the thrill was gone. He'd ridden in fifteen or twenty thousand races at tracks all over the country and the excitement he'd felt as a young man, that fantastic sense of lightness, of being in command, had dissipated. Now and then he got up for a big race, when the horses were classy and the competition tough, but mostly it was business as usual: workouts, the afternoon card, a quick shower, maybe dinner out, and then home to the ranch in Marin County where his kids were waiting. Often they were asleep by the time he got there, and they were always asleep when he left before dawn, and it upset him sometimes not to see more of them.

Mahorney didn't set out to become a jockey. His friends kept telling him he was the right size to ride (this was true of many jocks), but he knew nothing about racing and even less about horses. He was twenty years old, ambitionless, and working as a produce clerk in a Thrifty Mart store in Los Angeles when an acquaintance, a man who owned horses, offered to get him a job as a ranch hand at the Dandy Bar Ranch in Stockton, California. Mahorney turned in his lettuce heads and packed his bags. The Dandy Bar was a quarter-horse outfit and there

Mahorney cleaned stalls, groomed and curried and learned to ride. The ranch work suited him. He'd been born and raised in Washington, D.C., and in Stockton he encountered for the first time a fullness of life he'd been missing elsewhere, horses foaling, growing, running, dying. California got to him and soon he was wearing jeans, boots, and a cowboy hat around town, surrendering to the West. Later he would add the obligatory pickup truck.

His debut as a jockey came in a quarter-horse race at Pomona in 1962. Quarter horses are bred primarily for speed, and their races, which proceed from point to point with about as much intricacy as a bullet moving toward a target, seldom cover more than 870 yards. A jockey can do only two things to expedite matters, get his horse out of the gate quickly and keep him running straight. Mahorney did both of them well. In 1964 he graduated to thoroughbreds and broke his maiden on Mark Ye Royal. Trainers liked him because in addition to his riding skills he was bright and articulate and could supply them with much-needed information about their stock. Horses perform differently under pressure than they do in morning workouts, and if a jockey is attentive he can detect problems that might otherwise go undetected. He knows if his mount is laboring or breathing improperly or lugging in or out or being spooked by shadows. Mahorney, intelligent and English-speaking (speaking only Spanish could be a drawback for aspiring riders), was adept at communicating. He was also tougher than the average bugboy and wouldn't let older riders push him around during a race. They were notorious, these older jocks, for taking advantage of rookies whenever they could. They'd roar into a turn behind some bug and yell, "Get out of my way, I'm in trouble, the horse is going down," and when the terrified bug responded by taking up on the reins and moving away from the rail, they'd whisk through the hole he'd left behind, smiling all the while.

By 1965 Mahorney's career was in orbit. After being the leading apprentice at Santa Anita, he led all riders at both Aqueduct and Arlington Park; he made the transition from apprentice to journeyman with ease and finished second in the standings at Hollywood Park. He was floating along inside the jockey's dream bubble, with clothes, cars, girls, and money to burn, but already he was thinking a little too much. Success bothered him in some ways—it had come too simply, almost without effort—and he was beginning to realize that riding horses was a job like any other. It was a good job, better than juggling cucumbers at two bucks an hour, but the business aspects of it and the increasing demands on his time were disillusioning.

In the fall he returned to Arlington Park. There, at the start of the meet, he rode four winners in three days and appeared ready to dominate the ranks again. One night he was driving home in his new Bonneville and saw another car at the top of the hill he was ascending suddenly cross over the divider line on to his side of the road. It hit him head-on at sixty miles an hour. The kid driving it had passed out, and in the rolling softness of his stupor landed unharmed, but Mahorney woke up in the hospital with two broken knees. For the next few months he was flat on his back, staring at the ceiling.

"I'm afraid you'll never ride again, Bill," the doctor said, sounding like an actor in some TV movie, but Mahorney refused to accept the prognosis. As soon as he could get out of bed, he started working on his legs. Before long he was walking with crutches and then without them. He had trouble with disintegrating cartilage and slippage in the joints, but eventually he was strong enough to give riding another try. Instead of going to Arlington or Aqueduct he went to Golden Gate. Maybe he told himself he'd ship up to the big leagues again when he was fit, but this never happened. His knees were too fragile. Over the next decade the pain in his left knee increased and he could feel bones rubbing together, pinching the nerves. In 1976 he underwent surgery again. The doctors gave him an artificial joint of steel and plastic and told him he might be crippled for life, but this time he hardly even listened.

Lying there in the sun on the roof with his scarred knees in evidence Mahorney had the look of someone on the verge of satisfaction. Something in his attitude reminded me of gentlemen relaxing after dinner, grandfathers loosening their vests and lighting up cigars. No doubt it had taken him years to reconcile what he could do now with what he'd done in the past, and with his dreams, but he seemed pleased to be where he was, a star of the second magnitude at a track twice removed from the Ideal. He had to ride more often to make the same amount of money he'd made as a bug, but there was the consolation of those thirty-six acres in Marin. He was no longer so tough on himself, no longer so critical, although sometimes without warning the old anxiety snuck up and ambushed him. Just the other night, he said, he'd been driving home after the races when suddenly he'd gotten tense and angry, for no reason at all.

V

Back by Headley's barn one afternoon I heard the sound of a sewing machine and followed it into a small shop located at the extreme south end of the shedrow. A man with thick graying hair, Chuck Herndon, was working on some blinkers he'd designed to help trainers cut their expenses. The cloth hood featured Chicago eye screws around the eyeholes so that trainers could detach and replace the plastic blinker cups without having to replace the cloth, too. This was advantageous because different horses needed their vision adjusted in different ways. Some required only a half- or quarter-cup, just a sliver of the world obliterated. Herndon charged thirty-five dollars for the blinkers. He also made pennants and horse blankets, splitting the work load with his wife, but his major piece of merchandise was racing silks. Bolts of brilliant cloth, scarlet, chartreuse, shocking pink, hung from rollers behind his head. The shop was called *Colors by Herndon.*

Silks were first introduced at Newmarket racecourse in England in October 1762 for the purpose of identifying horses and jockeys during a race. Nineteen owners participated: seven dukes, one marquis, four earls, one viscount, one lord, two baronets, and three commoners. They all chose different colors, with the exception of two blues, sky and garter, but reached accord on their choice of cap, the black velvet one favored by huntsmen. These days, Herndon said, silks were made of nylon, though an occasional special order came in. He bought his material, a heavy-duty weave used in flags and bunting, from a wholesaler in Los Angeles. He charged between sixty-five and seventy-five dollars per set and for an additional fee would provide design consultation, helping owners pick an emblem or motif. His designs were often complex and made visual jokes. He showed me a photo of a shirt with a ferocious-looking tiger on the back, above the words "Big John Wong." "Wong's five feet tall and wears a cowboy hat," he said, "and I made those silks in the Year of the Tiger." I asked him how he liked the work. "Beats selling soap for Procter & Gamble," he said.

VI

Emery Winebrenner had hit a big exacta, four figures, and he was papering the Home Stretch with fifty-dollar bills. He bought drinks for Richard Labarr and for Labarr's two clients and for

Bob Ferris, who was drunk and shoeless, and for anybody else who expressed the tiniest desire for something liquid. When I came in he paid for my beer and told me five or six one-liners in rapid succession, all of them terrible, and then launched into a longer joke about a man who walked into a bar carrying his son. The poor boy had no arms or legs or appendages of any sort but he could speak just the same, and when his dad set him down he asked for a whiskey. As soon as he took a sip, *pop,* he sprouted an arm. *Terrific,* the boy thought. He ordered another drink and *pop,* sprouted another arm, and kept drinking and sprouting until he was fairly smashed and almost complete. All he needed now was a penis, so he ordered another drink but this time, *poof,* everything disappeared, each of his new limbs, and he was reduced once again to his pristine limbless state.

"You get it?" Emery asked, his eyes twinkling.

"Get what?"

"The moral of the story."

I thought it over but the moral escaped me.

Emery laughed. "Always quit when you're a head," he said. Then he slapped the bar. "Get it? *Always quit when you're ahead.*"

"Can't find my shoes, Emry," Ferris said.

"Keep looking. They must be here somewhere."

"Where'd you hide 'em, Emry?"

Emery winked. "I don't think anybody hid them, Bob."

An argument was going on in a booth along the wall. Jay Jsames, one of Labarr's riders, was telling another man who wore only gym shorts and sneakers that he, Jsames, was the fastest jockey at Golden Gate and probably in the nation. "I can fly," he said. Jsames was maybe twenty years old but he had flash. He put his ego out front, as a man might set his limbless son upon a bar, and played with it, half-seriously. He claimed to have had a brief career as a prizefighter, scoring several knockouts, and to have acted in movies, Hollywood movies, but more than anything else, he loved to ride. Labarr was getting him a few mounts, but it would be July before he held the reins of an animal who could really run. In the meantime he worked hard and cruised around in a Cadillac decorated with little American flags and threw down the gauntlet whenever his speed of foot was challenged.

Outside it was still warm; the air was choked with particulates. A phantasmagoric smog-set was occurring over the Bay and the clouds were riddled with agonized hues. Labarr paced off about seventy-five yards along the sidewalk, which was deserted at this time of day, and marked a finish line with Jsames's shirt. Jsames and his opponent, Ed, loosened up, touching their toes and running in place.

"You cheap speed, boy," Ed said.

"We'll see," said Jsames.

Then the money appeared. It jumped out of pockets in fat exacta rolls, and various people made book on the spot. No odds were given; it was even up all the way. Labarr, no doubt to be sporting, laid twenty on Ed, and Emery countered with twenty on Jsames. He kept saying what a crazy wonderful mixed-up racetrack thing this was to do. A dispute arose over how to start the race, how to make it fair for both runners, but this was solved ingeniously when a truck driver sitting behind the wheel of a horse van across the street offered to hit his horn as a signal. Jsames dropped down into a sprinter's stance, his fingers touching the pavement, and Ed stood quietly next to him, one foot ahead of the other and his arms dangling at his side. When the horn sounded, they took off full speed down the sidewalk. For forty yards they were even and then Jsames pulled slowly away, winning by a reasonable margin.

"You cheated," Ed said. "Let's do it again."

There was another round of heated wagering. This time Jsames won by a good ten yards, and on the way back to the starting line he needled the older man.

"Maybe you're a router," he said. "You sure don't belong in sprints."

"One more time," Ed said. His thigh muscles were twitching uncontrollably.

I watched the greenbacks go round. In five minutes Labarr had lost forty dollars and Emery had won forty, but I couldn't tell the difference by their expressions. This was how it went among racetrack gypsies. Their attitude toward money differed from most people's. Millions passed through the pari-mutuel windows every day and was rerouted in part, but the gypsies knew that nobody's life was ever changed. You could be ahead for a day, two days, a week, an entire meet, but sooner or later you lost. That Transformation Pie was still cooling on the windowsill, just out of reach. Money was paper, a government contrivance, something accountants and brokers pursued, but for gypsies it was useful only to keep score, to prove that for once you'd outsmarted horses, trainers, fixers, corporate thugs, and Trickster Process, forced a freeze on events, and imposed your own sense of continuity on the afternoon's card. What could you possibly buy with your winnings? You could buy *anything,* the answer went, so why bother? Anything was nothing. You could get credit against your paycheck at the Home Stretch, and the cafeteria food was cheap, and tack rooms were free, so what good was money? You couldn't hold on to it, that much was certain. Sooner or later you gave it back or spent it or had it taken away or woke up dead.

Jsames breezed home in the third race and we went back inside for drinks.

"I still don't believe it," Ed said, rubbing his quivery thighs. "I don't understand it at all."

"You better believe it," Jsames said cockily. "You ain't never gonna beat anybody fast as me."

Ed knew this was true and he withdrew for a moment to consider other games in which age and technique might grant him an edge. Finally he hit on something and looked much happier.

"You know that whorehouse in Oakland?" he asked with a grin.

"I heard about the place."

"Well, then, I'll tell you one thing you're not gonna beat me at."

"Do tell," said Jsames.

"Let's you and me go over there," Ed said. His grin took on beatific aspects. "We go in there, see who can make it last. I go all night long. You know what I mean, my man? I mean *all night long*."

VII

For six weeks of the meeting my betting ledger looked like this:

	Stake:	$500	
Week One:	372	(−128)
Week Two:	336	(− 36)
Week Three:	295	(− 41)
Week Four:	487	(+192)
Week Five:	522	(+ 35)
Week Six:	478	(− 44)

I attributed my rotten start to confusion, and Week Four's big winnings to being *in touch,* but otherwise what I had in hand was a record of breaking even.

Breaking even, how I hated those words! They were the province of coupon clippers, gas hoarders, voyeurs, of the apothecary Landucci, who bemoaned the fact that during a *festa* women and children had witnessed a stallion servicing a mare. Sexless Landucci, Landucci the scrimper of *soldi,* Landucci who probably played only favorites when the Florentine *palio* was run. What good would it do me to break even? Coyotes didn't break even, they went for broke. Money had little to do with what I was seeking, that much I'd learned, but I still thought it would indicate a failure of nerve if I went home with my stake intact. I felt trapped in The Grand Flat Middle, in Omaha, in Dubuque, with the corn silk of irresolution threaded in my hair.

My problem was epidemic among small-time gamblers. When you're playing with limited cash—twenty dollars was a big bet for me, the sixty I'd laid on Bushel Ruler more than a tenth of my original capital—it's difficult to win decisively, i.e., in quantities large enough to inflate the ego. A two-dollar bettor can pick four or five winners and if they're favorites show a profit of less than twenty dollars. Knowing you've been right four or five times and that what you win is indeed determined by what you wager somehow doesn't compensate for what seems an unjust return on your investment. So small-timers make the mistake, as I was beginning to do, of shopping around for long shots. Too often I passed up horses I liked because their odds were short, eight to five, even two to one, and bet instead second or third favorites on the outside chance they'd improve enough to win. They seldom did. Then, too, I was getting bored, in need of larger shocks, riskier endeavors, to obtain the results (adrenaline rushes, accelerated heartbeat) I'd always gotten freely as a casual bettor. Seeing the same jockeys every day, seeing them ride horses I'd seen run before, seeing the same races over the same distances carded in the same way . . . I was like a man who's lost the feel for his wife's thighs, for sparks.

So I decided like so many plungers before me to up the ante. I would bet less frequently (no more crazy two-dollar show tickets on forty-to-one shots who looked good in the paddock; they added up) but in higher units. A twenty-dollar bet on an eight-to-five horse produced a not unreasonable payoff. Also, I would concentrate my bets on a group of trainers I knew would send their horses to post fit and well-meant: Martin, Jenda, Hixon, Brinson, Olen Battles, Gilbert, Taylor, Walsh, and a few others. And I would stop playing the outside posts in sprints (I kept doing this, in violation of everything I knew) except under special circumstances. If I could do all these things, I thought I still might be able to show a profit.

VIII

The next day I got some news from home. Out at the dam site "progress" was being made. The Corps of Engineers' bulldozers were working round the clock, plugging up nature with anal fervor, and we'd even had our first suicide, some poor young woman who'd jumped off the bridge that had been built over the basin to be dammed. Her free-fall into dust and wild flowers struck me as a wholly appropriate symbol of a more general demise, of the specific sliding into the mass. The town's planning commission, chaired by a realtor, was busily amending the general plan, changing agricultural zoning to residential or commercial to accommodate the developers and carpetbaggers who were lining up along the avenues; on the plaza we now had a T-shirt store and a jewelry store and a store that sold candles, macrame, patchouli oil, incense, roach clips, and sensitive photographs of the very land parcels that were being rezoned. The tack shop was gone, and so was Buck's 311 Club and Western Auto, and the hardware store had been replaced by a "theme" restaurant whose owners apparently hoped to attract tourists with a clever arrangement of wine casks, wine bottles, and waitresses in short-skirted burgundy-colored uniforms. I thought of Piero di Cosimo in his vine-sheltered cottage. Of him the art historian Panofsky had written, "he considered the age in which he lived as depraved not by a willful departure from primaeval contentment, much less by a Fall from Grace, but only by the over-sophistication of a cultural development that had forgotten where to stop."

IX

Because the fair meetings would soon be starting, certain incompetent riders were already hustling trainers for future assignments at rinks in Santa Rosa and Vallejo.

"I thought maybe with the fairs coming up you might give me a mount," one such jockey said to a trainer. "I thought you might throw me a bone."

"Son, if you knew what kind of bones I had back at the barn you wouldn't want me to throw you one."

"You don't think they'd do much for my innards, eh?"

"No, I don't," said the trainer, rubbing a nose brutalized by Demon Rum. "Besides, I like you. You're my pal. If I ride you, I'll get on your case. Then you won't be my friend any more. I need friends more than I need jockeys."

Bob Hack walked by on his morning rounds and I joined him for a while. Ever since long-striding Ivan had dumped me into his lap, Hack had been kind to me, which came as no surprise. Everybody said he was a Nice Guy. They said it almost involuntarily whenever Hack's name was mentioned. "Gee, he's a nice guy," they'd say, or "Bob Hack? Helluva nice guy," and I began to wonder if Hack had some terrible secret they were trying to hide, in the way a small town pulls itself together to shield the village idiot. But no, it was just that Hack was . . . nice. He inspired awe because he was defying gravity. Nice guys were supposed to finish last, but there stood Hack as evidence to the contrary. The notion that niceness, perhaps even *goodness,* could be translated into greenbacks seemed to give people on the backstretch a spiritual lift. When Hack strolled by their barn they'd step out, smile shyly, and wave before returning to whatever sordid and nasty business they were perpetrating inside.

But Hack, when asked, credited his success to perseverance. "It looks so easy," he said, almost with a sigh, stopping to talk to a trainer who wanted Richie Galarsa to ride a nice filly of his but was confused about where to enter her. Hack took out his notebook and a well-thumbed Condition Book, its green cover falling off, and after consulting his sources advised the trainer to run the filly in the sixth race on Tuesday. "So far that's a weak field," he said. "You want me to enter her for you?" Agents often performed this service, saving trainers time. The trainer nodded and tapped Hack's shoulder gratefully. "Thanks a million, Bob," he said.

Hack was expert at accommodating his clients. He had the comfortable feel of old shoes, but this was somewhat deceptive. He was always scouting for business, even when he appeared to be just having a chat with another agent. I never saw him standing still. Instead he moved about in balletic little arcs and pirouettes, up on the balls of his feet, his eyes peering over shoulders, around the crowns of caps, looking for somebody he'd been meaning to contact. His connections were extensive, forged over almost thirty years on the backstretch, beginning when his father, then a foreman for trainer Bill Molter, got him a job rubbing horses. After a brief impractical stint as a trainer—his "stable" consisted of a few cheap nags with names like Overhead—Hack graduated to agenting.

From the start he represented good riders, Charlie Tohill,

Bobby Jennings, but with a growing family at home he needed a steady paycheck, so he began working afternoons, and still does, as a pari-mutuel clerk. This was his insurance, his hedge against catastrophe. The agent game was very risky, with suspensions, injuries, malice, relative popularity, and racing luck affecting your income, and Hack had almost quit on more than one occasion. Once during a low period, when his jockeys were cold, he'd taken a job selling tack at a backstretch shop. But he hated the sense of enclosure, of being in an *office,* and after a year and a half of self-inflicted torture he was back beating the shedrows for mounts. Now he was sitting pretty. Galarsa was live and Muñoz was steady, and Hack's ten percent share of their earnings would more than compensate him for his earlier shuffling. He liked being out in the morning, making his rounds, and he enjoyed the company of his peers, or most of them, anyway. "There's only one guy I don't like," he said. "I don't like the way he does business." I knew whom he meant. Nobody liked the agent in question because he was a crook. He tried to bribe trainers, telling them he'd bet a hundred for them if they used his boy on a hot horse in a stakes race, and he stepped on everybody's toes in the process.

Like most agents Hack had a parental attachment to his riders. When jockeys faltered, their agents took them in, giving them bed and board and steering them away from fast chickies and uranium deals in Pensacola, Florida. Hack was especially concerned about Galarsa, who was making big money now but might not get mounts so easily when he'd lost the bug. "I hope he's banking some of it," Hack would say wearily, the many lines in his face becoming abruptly visible. One of his best young riders, Juan Gonzalez, had been killed in a bad spill at the Pleasanton fairgrounds not so long ago, and Hack still flinched whenever Gonzalez was mentioned in his presence.

We stopped at the cafeteria for coffee and sat at a table with Jack Orloff, agent for Tony Diaz. Orloff, *aka* Camel Driver, *aka* the Rodent, had cultivated a style in contradistinction to Hack's quiet self-effacement. He wore faded denim outfits, gold neck-chains, and aviator sunglasses, while Hack kicked around in sneakers, khakis, and on windy days a baseball cap. Orloff's natural habitat would be some steamy enclave like Marina del Rey, but Hack was better suited to a backyard in Anytown, USA, with steaks sizzling on the grill and a cold brew in his hand. Orloff was lounging around because Diaz had just been set down for five days, and he offered some of Tony's mounts to Hack for Galarsa or Muñoz to ride. There was nothing curious about this gesture, except that when it happened, the agent dealing always traded down, reflecting once again the rigid stratification of the track. Diaz was more experienced and made more money than either of Hack's boys, so Orloff could dispense favors with a kind of *lèse majesté* to agents on the rung just below him. Sometimes friendship or sympathy cut through the strata, and an established agent helped out a younger associate. Orloff helped Rogelio Gomez's agent, *aka* the Vulture, perhaps because the kid had a dark tan and dark curly hair and wore modish clothes in a style similar to Orloff's.

While we were at the table, the Vulture swooped into the cafeteria with his arms outstretched, moving in circles around the table. Apparently he thought vultures were raptors, not carrion eaters, and he swooped down at the Rodent as though to attack.

"Hey, it's the Vulture," Hack said.

"I'm here to prey on rodents," the Vulture replied.

Orloff was unimpressed. "Did you do what I told you to do?" he asked.

"I did it."

"And did you get some mounts?"

"I got them."

"And what was it you said you'd do for me if I got you some mounts?"

The Vulture pretended to be puzzled. "What did I say?"

"What do you mean, 'What did I say?'" Orloff frowned. "How can you say that?"

Hack had other barns to visit, so we left the cafeteria and went down another shedrow. A hundred yards away I saw a big bony colt acting up. He'd just returned from a gallop and he was feeling good. He pranced along with that challenging winner's gait. Thoroughbreds are athletes and they probably share with other athletes the brief period of illumination that follows a satisfying workout. The parts of your body mesh so freely, with such perfection, that you seem made of light. Surely this colt was light-headed, tipsy on oxygen. He wouldn't go into his stall, and his groom, who was falling behind in his work, was getting impatient and losing control. The colt reared once, and the groom cursed and yanked on his reins. Then he reached for a shank. Horses on the hotwalker in front of the barn sensed that something was wrong and slowed their pace. The groom made a fearsome face and approached the colt, brandishing the shank, but still the cold wouldn't budge. The groom cursed loudly and lifted the shank and then the colt broke loose. He galloped along at full speed for about thirty-five yards, then stopped and looked around. He seemed to be confused and a little panicked, as though he hadn't understood where his resistance would lead him. Other grooms came out of their barns and talked to him, trying to keep him from damaging their stock. An old man with a long white beard, the birdnesty beard of a wizard, walked toward him, talking all the while in a gentle singsong voice, but when he had the reins almost in hand the colt took off again. He was moving faster now, out of a greater panic, making split-second turns to avoid equipment and grooms. I thought for sure he'd break an ankle. An exercise rider saw him coming and tried to head him, but the colt switched directions again, crossing over to the opposite side of the shedrow and galloping right toward us. I froze. Hack grabbed my arm and pulled me back under the shedrow roof. The colt passed within inches, close enough to draw a breeze under my chin. Two grooms were waiting for him at the end of the shedrow. They stood right in his path and waved their arms back and forth in semaphore. The colt kept right on coming, still galloping for all he was worth, and I thought the grooms would have to dive into the hay, but at the last possible second the colt pulled up. He flared his nostrils and shook his head around and began pacing in circles, giving himself over to containment again. A third groom took his reins, and he allowed himself to be led back to the barn. All the way back he pranced, raising his haunches high. I looked over at Hack, who was adjusting his baseball cap.

"I'm scared chickenshit of horses," he said.

X

Horses kept breaking loose in Florence, too, all the time, barreling riderless over the cobbles toward families dining in the streets, trashing furniture and scattering chicken bones and the bones of geese and pigeons, and driving small children up against the wall. Men rode off to war on horseback and when they returned, their brides met them at the chapel riding fine-looking chestnuts and bays. (Patriarchal tradition dictated, however, that a bride follow her new master home on foot after the ceremony.) Indeed, it was said in Florence that a husband who understood his wife "knew the trot of his mare." Before Lorenzo's marriage to Clarice Orsini, a tournament was held, and horses clashed as they clashed in Uccello's paintings. Horses were used for carrying mail and diplomatic pouches and notes of assignation, for transport and trade, for pleasure riding and hunting and leisurely trips to the countryside, and served in mute partnership on drunken revels and night raids, saving many a nobleman from certain death at the hands of a wrathful cuckold. Their manure mixed with the human excrement flowing in gutters to the Arno; their essence permeated the city.

XI

This was Pichi's big day. Headley had decided to run her over a distance of ground, a mile and a sixteenth. She'd never gone so far before, not at Del Mar or Hollywood Park, but she was running against a delicate field of maidens, fading beauties who'd already had ten chances to lose their virginity, and even a couple of the *Form*'s expert handicappers thought she might win. Hermis picked her first, and so did Handicap. In the consensus she ranked second behind Button Face, a funky little roan of no appreciable class. Everything seemed propitious, and then early on the morning of the race Jimmy Colaneri, the jockey, came by the barn to show off his swollen jaw. It was black-and-blue, the result of an impacted tooth. He told Headley in a mumble that he wouldn't be riding Pichi partly because of his toothache, but mostly because the stewards had just set him down for bumping another rider in the ninth race the day before. Colaneri felt bad, but Headley told him not to worry. At the same time Headley's brain was clicking wildly ahead in search of a replacement rider. He hated to lose Colaneri, who'd done such a good job last time out. Moreover, Colaneri had the bug, and his five-pound allowance would've meant a great deal to Pichi, especially in a route race. She was likely to sink under a heavier load.

But Headley couldn't find an available apprentice to his liking, and settled at last on Mel Lewis, a skillful rider who was sixty-two years old and a mighty favorite of the Golden Gate publicity department. Whenever reporters from surrounding newspapers dropped by for their semiannual visit, they were offered, as subject matter for feature stories, Lewis (human interest), Efa, the twelve-year-old horse (equine interest), Mahorney (the Bionic Man, scientific interest), Aragon (noble Peruvian), and the clubhouse chef (gourmet interest). When Steve Cauthen came north in 1977 to ride in the California Derby, he and Lewis were forced into posing together in a youth-and-age tableau, and in the ensuing photograph both jockeys look as though they've eaten too many burritos. Headley had faith in Lewis's ability to handle a finicky filly, but the added weight gave him pause. The Sandomirs expected a victory and now he wasn't sure Pichi would deliver.

"At least they're not crazy like some owners," he said. "They won't fire me if she loses. I had this one owner, he took his horse away from me after a claiming race because the horse didn't win by far enough. Can you imagine that? I had another owner, his horse was a router but he'd only let me run him in sprints. Then he'd yell at me when the horse lost."

"Why'd he do that?"

"Because he was crazy is why."

Bo was busy in Pichi's stall. He was combing her mane, drawing strands of it forward so they fell prettily between her eyes. I asked him how long she needed to rest between races.

"Depends," he said. "This time she only did rest six days. Next time, we'll have to rest her up ten, fourteen days, before she'll be ready."

"You remember Rob Bob, Bo?" Headley asked.

"Rob Bob was a nice kind of a horse."

"He used to run at the fairs. Rob Bob ran with less rest than any horse I ever saw. One time I saw him finish second on Friday and come back to win on Saturday. He must've been thirteen or fourteen, too."

"Rob Bob had forty-eight wins. Two more and he'd of made the Hall of Fame."

"How'd he die, Bo?"

"I think he cracked a bone. I think he just broke down."

Before the race I watched Headley in the paddock. Most trainers at Golden Gate didn't win often enough to be cavalier when their horses really had a shot, and Headley was a case in point. His tics and gestures were all exaggerated. He moved with the quirky precision of an instrument wound too tightly, performing under tension. He chain-smoked and chewed gum, popping the wad with his teeth, and stuttered more than usual. When Lewis entered the stall he introduced the jockey to the Sandomirs and then repeated, adding rhetorical flourishes, the instructions he'd given earlier: whip the horse left-handed and watch her in the gate. Lewis did a better job of acting than he'd done in the youth-and-age tableau. He crossed his arms, furrowed his brow, and let a rapt expression play across his features, as though committing Headley's words to memory.

The gate for the race was set up near the middle of the grandstand, and I had a fine view of Pichi going into the three hole. She made no complaint. In fact, she looked almost relaxed, turning this way and that to sniff at her opponents. Spring was a difficult season for fillies. "They's got other things on their minds besides racing," Bo told me once. A few days ago I'd seen a filly trying to invert the natural order by mounting a pony during the post parade. The horses in this race were showing similar signs of distress. When the gate snapped open Pichi took them by surprise. She broke slightly to the right but earlier than the others and had a head out on the lead. Immediately several jockeys who'd broken from outside posts began challenging the horses inside, hoping to sweep past them and take a position on the rail, and Lewis made a split-second decision to keep Pichi out front. He touched her lightly and she ran. The decision was questionable because it had demanded an expenditure of energy—speed—that might better have been saved for use later on, but Pichi appeared none the worse for wear. She trailed Bargain Belle, a filly with good early foot. Rounding into the first turn Lewis asked her and she came on to take the lead. She wasn't ahead by much, but she was ahead, and the sight was one I thought I'd never see. She was striding elegantly, gliding along, her legs fully extended, and for the first time she looked like a *racehorse,* a *thoroughbred,* an animal invented for the single purpose of *running,* her body geared precisely to the flow of the action and unfolding by perfect and apparently unlabored increments. When horses ran this way, I thought they must have no sense of competition, of other horses on their heels. They moved so gracefully forward in the matrix of their flesh that it was easy to forget, watching, that every stride exacted a price.

The first quarter went in .23.3, a creeping pace, perfect for platers, and I thought Pichi might have enough left to hold on. Going down the backstretch she was still gliding, and Lewis was just beginning to restrain her in an attempt to bank something against the future. He took back on the reins, lifted his butt off the saddle and let his weight settle down through his legs and rest more heavily on her. She dropped back to second. A few strides later she was third. I wanted to believe her retreat was tactical, but moments later Annie Get Your Gun, the favorite, came up to challenge. When she passed Pichi, the two horses were held briefly in juxtaposition and I could see how tired Pichi was. Her tail drooped and her gait was now awkward and out of rhythm. She looked like a battered club fighter coming out for the tenth round, wobbly-legged, not caring about winning any more, trying only to finish. She was all used up, and when Annie

Get Your Gun's tail waved in her face, she quit a little more. For her the race was like a series of debilitating body punches. Lewis wouldn't think of whipping her. She dragged home eighth, beating only a few cripples and Bargain Belle, who'd also bloomed too soon.

Although Lewis had made a costly error in judgment by asking Pichi too early in the race, drawing too heavily on her reserves, it was difficult to hold him responsible. Rating a horse is a complex affair, and to do it successfully a jockey must know his mount well. During the course of a race he has to decide how best to apportion a finite quality, his horse's speed, over the distance of ground to be covered. Moreover, he has to make adjustments in the rate of apportionment according to the rate at which the race evolves, within the context of its pace. His job is to correlate one notion of time with another and achieve synchronism. Here Lewis had failed. Pichi had never been a front-runner, and he was wrong to take her out on the lead. If she was ever to win she'd have to come from off the pace, making her move in the stretch, and the pace would have to be slow enough not to exhaust her.

I saw Headley later and he looked glum. He'd begun to think a terrible thing about Pichi, that she was a late-breaking sprinter, the sort of horse destined forever to lose because she burned up if pushed too early, and came on too late when saved for the stretch. "I don't know what's next," he said gloomily. Bo was unwrapping Pichi's legs. "She never was a router," he whispered, touching her ribs. "Look what a skinny son-of-a-bitch she is. How's a filly going to run that far when she don't eat?"

XII

Like the horses, Art Lobato let you know when he was feeling good. One afternoon he won a stakes race on Fleet's Delight, and after dismounting he jumped up and clicked his boot heels together in full view of the crowd. He did it again, and once more, then waved to the fans and disappeared into the Jockeys' Room. The stewards called down to scold him for showing off, but Lobato didn't care. He'd just earned eight hundred dollars doing what he loved. It was his biggest payday in a long time. Once he'd been a live rider with a purchase on the future, but now he was hustling for nickels and dimes. "I could go up to Portland and do fine," he told me once at the Home Stretch. "Lonnie Arterburn, he couldn't cut it at Golden Gate, but he's in the standings at Portland Meadows."

"So why don't you go?"

He shook his head. "I want to make it here."

For him it was a matter of pride. This was a quality shared by all jockeys, but it was particularly prominent in the smaller ones. They were caught in a curious bind. The minute they left the track, they were stripped of the extra dimension riding granted them and were stuffed back into the real parameters of their bodies. Out in the world, buying jeans in the boy's department of Macy's, they were just short men, strange children, and had the same problems of integration as tall basketball players and sensitive poets. Pride became a means of coping, a defense against the limits of the flesh.

Lobato's career had been affected by an accident similar to Bill Mahorney's. On April 13, 1974, he shattered his leg in fifteen places while working a mean two-year-old, Thunder's Roar, for Jake Battles. Battles planned to race the colt soon, and as a test he wanted him set down hard over five furlongs. He told Lobato to apply the whip whenever necessary. The colt resisted from the start, and Lobato hit him twice, knifing him on the flank. The third time he brought down the whip, Thunder's Roar ducked sharply to the left and broke through the infield railing. Lobato fell, rolled ten yards, and crashed into the base of the starter's stand, a big wooden structure on the grass. For a minute he lay still, staring at the sky. When he looked down he saw bones poking through his skin. A gateman ran over and tied some cardboard around his leg so the pieces wouldn't fall apart on the way to the hospital. Several operations were necessary before the bones finally began to knit; the episode consumed two years of Lobato's life and left him with a leg not much bigger around than his wrist. Gradually he built it up again, but he still walks with a barely detectable limp.

Listening to his story made me aware how tough it could be for jockeys to stay on top. A slip, a fall, a streak of bad luck, and down you tumbled to the bottom of the hill. Riding was a quicksilver occupation. Once you were known to have problems, however minor, they tended to become definitional. "I wish I had Lobato's head in a sound body," one trainer told me, making excuses. "Then I'd give him a ride." You heard such statements all the time, good deeds that perished on the tongue. What Lobato needed was not sentiment but a few decent mounts. He was almost thirty, and there were days when he wished he'd stayed with carpentry or electronics instead of trying to make it as a jockey. Soon the nightmares would begin, but for now, high on Fleet's Delight, he was optimistic. What could compare to winning a race on a horse who fit you truly? It felt like riding along on your instincts, like the best sex you ever had, and it confirmed you in a vision of self, even as hitting an exacta confirmed a gambler's sense of genius.

"I'm not quitting yet," Lobato said. "It took Merlin Volzke fifteen years to make it."

He told me about watching Cauthen ride in the California Derby. Cauthen was just a kid, slim and hairless, but he sat so still in the saddle you could balance a full glass of water on his head without spilling a drop. He rode effortlessly, with a silken effect, and Lobato had been very impressed. He knew he'd never approach Cauthen's stature, but the fact that Cauthen was around encouraged him, and he kept right on plugging, jogging from barn to barn instead of walking, hustling for mounts every morning, running in that funny way he had, hobbled a little, one leg shorter than the other.

XIII

So jockeys went about their business, visibly rising and falling, blown about by fate, pinfeathers in a Bay wind, and still there were those in the grandstand who held them accountable when the horse they were riding ran too slow. "You bum, Diaz," these mechanists shouted, "why the hell didn't you speed up on the turn?" Pistons, cylinders, combustion, racetracks as freeways, horses as semisophisticated machines. Jockeys as drivers, motorists. Winning as an exercise in downshifting, being in the right gear. "You let out the clutch too fast, Galarsa." Life as a giant V-8 engine, torpid, sluggish.

For me each race was a sentence written in an ongoing history, extending by virtue of its utterance the possibilities of speech. Handicappers as grammarians, frantically parsing. The sentences were familiar but appealingly varied, and the language of which they were the substance went backward and forward in time, recapitulating the past even as it posited the future. Jockeys provided the syntax, the structure, holding things together.

XIV

On Preakness Saturday I bumped into Arnold Walker at the clubhouse bar. He had forsaken his usual pin-striped suit for a dark-green Lacoste shirt and complementary trousers, and he had with him a "really terrific babe," June, who'd already caused a furor by trying to order a frozen daiquiri. June wanted Indigo Star to beat Affirmed. "That's such a beautiful name," she said. I was carrying a copy of Eddie Arcaro's ghost-written autobiography, *I Ride to Win,* and I told Arnold how Arcaro's life paralleled the lives of the jockeys I'd been talking to. He was small and everybody said he should be a jockey, so he got Pop Arcaro to take him to Latonia Downs, where he served an apprenticeship with trainer Roscoe Goose. It was a very Dickensian tale until Eddie hit the big time. Then anecdotes about Hollywood stars, junkets to Texas to inspect oil wells, and fishing vacations in Florida took over. Arnold wondered if a jockey would be strong enough to haul in a tarpon.

"Tarpons are killers," he said.

Around us a crowd had gathered and we seemed to be sailing as a body toward Baltimore, where the post parade at Pimlico was just beginning. I felt the press of warm scented flesh, and it seemed to mitigate the usual iciness of TV transmission. Affirmed and Alydar were decidedly not Laverne and Shirley. They looked dense, real, steeped in history. When they went to the gate, the crowd made a distinct humming sound and their juices flowed more quickly, raising the temperature and wafting perfume and clove-based cologne into the air. The flag went up. People pressed in more tightly still, a hip thrown against a stranger's hip, bonding like atoms in a molecule, losing themselves. This was the pivotal function of the event, of any legendary event, to draw the mind out of its turnings and point it toward some notion of the eternal, however false that notion might be.

Then they were off, in a shotgun burst of color, and I felt another forward surge, nerves set suddenly on edge. Track Reward went to the front, but Affirmed was right next to him and took over the lead coming out of the turn. He was running easily and Cauthen was sitting chilly. Jorge Velásquez held Alydar tight at the back of the pack, and the colt moved along step for step in a shadow dance to the pace Affirmed was making. That Alydar had power and would take his shot was never in doubt, but the *when,* the precise instant of release, kept us in suspense. Indigo Star was fifth at the half, and I looked over at June, whose hand rested in Arnold's back pocket, and saw her face powdered with hope, impossible hope. The horses rounded into the stretch and then Alydar was there, a length behind and coming, and then he was up and there and almost hooking Affirmed head to head. They moved in tandem toward the wire and Cauthen leaned forward and asked his colt, *Go baby,* mooching sweet nothings in his ear, and Affirmed responded and began to pull away. Velásquez set Alydar down, but the colt couldn't quite make it. Cauthen had done an expert job of rating, and Affirmed had a little more left at the end, a dollop more in the cup, just enough to stretch out and cross the wire in front. The tension began to subside, and as it passed I could feel people coming down, as they might from sex or drugs. It was odd to see flushed cheeks and satisfied smiles beaming through the familiar stale cloud of smoke.

After the race I listened to Cauthen and heard in his voice the melodious innocence of all young jockeys, an accent full of southern syrup but characteristic even in the west. I went outside to sit by the Bay. My racing high had not yet dissipated and I was able to sit still on the rocks without worrying about what would happen next. But this was solved for me anyway when I saw a big rat slink from a crevice and drag its slithery tail over moss and potato chip bags, destroying in the process the brief ascendance into the legendary I had so enjoyed.

Chapter Eight

Ruling Don was the first horse I ever saw die. He broke down in May, on a beautiful morning with the sun shining and all the touts and trainers along the rail talking of summer, of county fairs and smaller tracks like the one up the coast in Ferndale, where the breeze blew lightly in off the ocean and kept things cool. I was standing among them when I heard the sharp sudden gunlike sound of bone breaking and looked up and saw a horse begin to falter. This was Ruling Don. He'd been working five furlongs fast, inside on the rail, running well, but then his right front leg had broken abruptly in half and he'd gone out of control. His shin and hoof flopped about in the dirt, held in place by a hinge of skin, and he pitched forward as though he'd been pushed down a flight of stairs, with the same panicky flailing. When he stumbled past the main gate, I saw that he was running now on three legs and a stub of bone, hop-stepping toward oblivion. He couldn't quite stop himself. His limbs worked of their own accord and carried him forward along the curve of energy expended, downward in compliance with gravity.

Art Lobato was riding him. He was pulling up hard on the

reins, but Ruling Don kept stumbling forward, threatening to fall. Lobato knew if the horse fell he'd likely be crushed, so he slipped his feet from the stirrups and bailed out. He hit the track with a thud, then gathered himself into a fetal ball, arms crossed over his knees, and looked back to see if he'd be trampled by other horses still coming. He was lucky, though, the horses had been taken in hand or steered wide or yanked to a halt, and he was able to scuttle crabwise under the rail to the safety of the infield grass. He was wearing a strapped red T-shirt and for a moment I thought the dark stains on his chest were blood. But he was just sweating. His face had no color in it. He looked pale and old.

About twenty yards down the track Ruling Don tripped to a stop without losing his balance. He was breathing hard and looking around in a bewildered way, tottering on his unbalanced legs. Every now and then he tried to take a step forward but managed only to lurch a few inches and shift his weight. Somebody ran over and took his reins and rubbed his forehead, while Slaughterhouse Red called the Corporation Yard and told the maintenance boys to send over a van in a hurry. An exercise rider walked past me, wiping viciously at his eyes. "It always gets to me when that happens," he said. "Don't matter how often I see it, it always gets to me." A few trainers nodded in agreement and bitched among themselves about the condition of the strip, but they did this every morning. *It's a crime for horses to have to run over shit like this,* they said, and picked up pebbles and smoothed over cockles and hoofmarks as though such hasty minuscule improvements would make things better.

"There's just too goddam many sore horses running these days," one man said.

The man next to him spat. "So what else is new," he said.

Bob Hess, who'd once trained Ruling Don, stood with his back to the track and said that he'd thought the horse might have had some problems, but nothing serious, nothing bad enough to break him down.

Five minutes later the van drove onto the strip, and two men got out and unlatched the back door. They lowered a ramp for Ruling Don and coaxed him along, but after three tentative steps he quit. The pain was too great. Blood trickled down from his knee, and he twisted his head around. His bewilderment seemed to increase, spiraling into fear. The men got behind him and locked their hands over his tail, forming a sling with their arms, and they were joined by Lobato and Gerry Danbrook, the horse's trainer, and Mike McRae, a veterinarian. Together they pushed, and Ruling Don proceeded reluctantly up the ramp, dragging the exposed bone over ridges of corrugated metal. It made a scraping noise and had the effect on some bystanders of chalk squeaking on a blackboard. When the horse was inside at last the men latched the doors behind him and drove over to the Corporation Yard.

Danbrook phoned the horse's owner, John Schipani, who'd claimed Ruling Don from Hess for twelve thousand five hundred dollars. Danbrook was apprehensive because Schipani had suggested the claim, and it was clear now that he had purchased damaged goods. He gave Schipani a brief medical report. Ruling Don had fractured a cannon bone and exploded a fetlock joint, but his leg could be repaired in a fairly common operation. The surgery would have to be done elsewhere, though, because the emergency facilities at Golden Gate were minimal at best. In all probability, Danbrook said, Ruling Don would never race again and would have to be destroyed. There was really no reason to keep him alive. He couldn't race, he was a gelding and hence useless at stud, and besides, Schipani had no insurance to cover the costs of surgery. Insurance was never a guarantee that a horse would be saved, anyway. Often enough owners had marginally injured stock put down just to collect a premium. Most cheap horses were worth more dead than alive.

So Danbrook passed along his decision to McRae, who set about preparing his "euthanasia solution." Its primary component was phenobarbital. The drug acted directly on the central nervous system, shutting down all sensory input. Sometimes McRae administered curare before the phenobarb to deaden a horse's muscles and prevent any radical reactions, the organism's involuntary kicking and rearing, but Ruling Don was in shock and behaving calmly. McRae slipped in the needle, and the horse overdosed almost immediately. His muscles quivered, his eyes glazed over, and he dropped to the ground. The appropriate forms were signed. A representative of the track had already telephoned Clarence Pementel of Mission San Jose. Pementel had an arrangement with Golden Gate that entitled him to all unwanted carcasses, the offal of a season's racing.

Back by the main gate some heavy-handed joking was going on. Lobato told Bob Hack that Richie Galarsa was supposed to have worked the horse for Danbrook, and that he, Lobato, had only been doing Richie a favor. Hack grimaced. Then a dour little groom with sunken eyes strolled by and seeing Lobato said, "Hey, Artie, I got this good horse for you to ride. This Ruling Don."

Lobato forced a smile—his lips trembled at the corners—and said, "I'm not riding any Ruling Don, man. Nobody's riding that horse any more. Ruling Don, he's dead."

II

Ruling Don's history was brief and melancholy and barely long enough to fill a dossier:

Chestnut gelding, three years old. Ancestry undistinguished, Windsor Ruler out of Señorita Cevole. Raced a total of eleven times. One first, two seconds, a third. Earned about four thousand dollars. Debut at Agua Caliente, Tijuana, Mexico, August 28, 1977. Finished eighth. Ran four more times at Caliente before breaking his maiden on October 16, going a mile in 1:37.3. Showed evidence of a good stretch kick. Potential talent. Shipped to Bay Meadows in November, ran a promising fourth in a claiming race. Ran again at Bay Meadows on November 25 and was claimed by Bob Hess for sixteen thousand. Raced first time for Hess, in owner Pergakis's colors, on December 17, stepping up to allowance company with Tony Diaz riding. Apparently serious bid, but finished dismal seventh on muddy track, sixteen lengths behind. Indication of leg problems, causing perceptual transference. No longer a stakes-caliber horse, no longer quite so valuable. Reduced to commodity status. Rested three months before racing again, then ran at Golden Gate on March 16, 1978. Seventh by five and a half lengths. Ran next a month later for a fourteen-thousand-dollar price tag. Appeared to have the race in hand, but jockey, Raul Caballero, was forced very wide on the turn and gave up too much ground. Finished fifth, returned to the barn tired. Entered again on April 22. Price tag dropped this time to twelve thousand. Good start, tired in the stretch, finished third. Claimed by Gerry Danbrook. Never raced again.

III

Gerry Danbrook was just returning from a gallop when I caught up with him at his barn. He swept down from the saddle and walked briskly toward the shedrow, strutting like an adjutant. A Snoopy-the-Red-Baron decal was glued to his riding helmet. "I call this Bad News Week," he said. First he'd lost two nice horses, saw them claimed away, then Ruling Don had gone out and busted a leg. Danbrook's stable had been reduced to a rudimentary three head, but he was playing it tough. Toughness was a quality he admired, a manly quality, and when he ordered his teen-age groom to wash down his mount, he did so with authority.

This wasn't the first time Danbrook had suffered through a spate of bad news. Back in 1976 a trainer down south was about to ship up a string of horses for him to handle, but Golden Gates' janitors had gone on strike and closed the track, which soured the deal. So Danbrook, with nothing to do, had taken a vacation in Toronto, his hometown. The trip was a bust, though, when his wife phoned from California to say she was leaving him. Bad news was part of the game, part of *life,* and Danbrook refused to buckle under to it. He'd been around race-tracks since he was fifteen. He was thirty-one now, a compact curly-haired man with a fashionable mustache and a chest pushed forward by ambition. He wanted desperately to be known as a winner, so he was less than anxious to discuss Ruling Don.

"Come into my office, we'll have a cup of coffee," he said, leading me into a tack room equipped with a coffeemaker and several cans of Yuban. On the wall, a poster showing hand-holding lovers skipping out of a misty landscape advised us that whenever we thought things were done, there was always something more to do. Apparently this was another aspect of Danbrook's present credo. Twice before he'd left racing, once to take a trip to Asia and once to go back to college—he wanted to be a pilot—and this time around he was determined to stick it out.

I asked him to tell me about Ruling Don.

"Ah, you know," he said, looking at the floor, "the horse had problems."

"What kind of problems?"

"He was sore. His legs weren't in such good shape."

"Was he running on phenylbutazone?"

Danbrook frowned. "Most of the horses here run on bute." He poured out some coffee.

"What did Schipani say when you told him?" I asked.

"John Schipani's a class guy. He understands these things. I already learned a lot from him."

For a while we sipped our coffee and talked more generally about racing, and then Danbrook got fidgety.

"Listen," he said, "I don't bullshit my owners. That horse wasn't very sound, but that's the chance you take in claiming. You're bound to get some bad ones. I'm not going to cry about it. Before, I used to listen to too many people. People are always trying to screw you up. The other day, Art Hirsch, he told me if I ran my horse Pobjoy for eighty-five hundred instead of twelve-five he'd claim him. Used to be that would get to me. I'd be up all night thinking. Not any more. I ran Pobjoy for eighty-five, he won, nobody claimed him."

"What would've happened with Ruling Don?"

"He would've been a useful horse. Nothing special. I would've kept him till he wasn't useful, then tried to get rid of him. That's how it goes."

We stood outside and watched the groom working. Mike McCrae passed by and Danbrook kidded him about all the business he'd been sending McCrae's way. McCrae was in a hurry and didn't stay long. His practice, private but licensed and supervised by the state, was a floating one, and he went from barn to barn, working to keep the walking wounded from falling apart, squeezing a last race or two out of nags bound for greener pastures.

"You know," Danbrook said reflectively, "I used to think

there were secrets to the game. But there aren't any, really. To win you need good horses. You've got to take good care of them and run them in the right spots. But secrets? No way."

He told the groom to saddle Low Lie, and when the boy brought out the horse he mounted up. I felt uncomfortable talking to him while he was on horseback. Low Lie seemed to give him a swelling sense of pomp, and I understood why soldiers loved to pose for equestrian portraits, sitting grand and tall with a thousand pounds of speed between their legs. We shook hands and Danbrook set off, marking a slow course between the shedrows. Then he stopped suddenly and turned around in the saddle, posed just like a statue, a John Hawkwood of the backstretch.

"You know what it really is?" he shouted. "It's balls! That's all. *Balls!* If you don't have 'em the guys who do'll step all over you. Balls, that's what it takes."

He touched his boots to Low Lie's ribs and rode off.

IV

In the late nineteenth century, aminopyrine, a derivative of pyrazolon, was introduced into medicine as an antipyretic, or fever-reducing agent, and soon found additional favor both as an analgesic and anti-inflammatory. Researchers later discovered that aminopyrine had potentially fatal bone-marrow toxicity, and the drug has since disappeared from the therapeutic scene in the United States, replaced in part by its congener (of the same genus, having similar properties) phenylbutazone, a compound first used to make aminopyrine soluble. Phenylbutazone, tradename Butazolidin, has anti-inflammatory properties akin to but stronger than those of aspirin, although as an analgesic and antipyretic it is of limited value. Among horses the compound

is used in the treatment of rheumatism, arthritis, and musculo-
skeletal disorders. It works primarily by inhibiting the biosyn-
thesis of prostaglandins, those diverse and bewildering hormones
that, in some instances, are the cause of inflammation.

On the backstretch, phenylbutazone is nicknamed "bute," a
word pronounced with the same crisp technological fervor as
disco or *module*. Bute is modern, efficient, an equine penicillin
capable of transforming sore horses into competitors; seventy-
five percent of the stock at Golden Gate took it regularly,
either orally or by injection.* The drug whose use it was sup-
planting, cortisone, a steroid, had awesome side effects including
pituitary upset, hormonal imbalance, fluid retention, retardation
of the natural healing processes, and, maybe, tumors. Despite
these drawbacks about thirty percent of the stock still raced on
cortisone (often in tandem with bute), and if you looked closely
you could identify them in the paddock by the needle marks
around their knees and hoofs. Sometimes cortisone collected in
the body, bulging out here and there in lumpy pockets, and
needed to be drained. It was a frightening compound and any
alternative to it had to be deemed a pharmacological breakthrough, as well as an advance in humane treatment.

But phenylbutazone also had problems. They were less visible,
more insidious, falling into familiar patterns of abuse. Bute
worked so well to alleviate soreness, banishing aches as easily
as Valium unraveled tensions, that it was given almost randomly
at the first sign of stiffness, even to lightly raced two-year-olds
who might in the past have been rested until they were fit.
Once the pattern started it was difficult to stop. Vets had little
control over the specific application of the drug because they

* Oxyphenbutazone, Tandearil, a bute derivative, is often used in its
stead. Tandearil has nearly identical properties, but causes less gastric
irritation.

were dependent on trainers for their livelihood. They had to be accommodating. If Trainer X demanded bute for a sore filly, then Vét Y usually prescribed it, even if he considered it unnecessary or counterindicated, on the assumption that if he didn't, another vet would. The California Horse Racing Board's veterinary representative, Dr. Jay Hoop, supervised drug use on the grounds at Golden Gate, but since the Board believed bute to be relatively harmless when given in accordance with certain guidelines, Hoop had little actual say unless these guidelines were transgressed. Even bute's efficiency had negative attributes, especially for those marginal horses who were always sore and couldn't move very well without drugs. When they ran on bute, they moved freely, but they couldn't feel the pain associated with inflammation. They were running uninformed, with their warning systems shut down, and they tended to exert undue and dangerous pressure on sensitive joints and muscles. They ran, in effect, on chemicals when they should've been resting or put out to pasture, and it seemed to me that more horses than ever before were breaking down in the doped and struggling manner of poor Ruling Don.

V

Jay Hoop, DVM, a tall gentlemanly figure in his sixties, dressed nattily in checked slacks, blue blazer, and Dobbs hat, had his office in the receiving barn, a rotundalike structure with numbered stalls all along its interior circumference. The barn was painted dark red, and restrictive signs were plastered near the entrance. A security guard in rent-a-cop gray was posted nearby to make sure that unauthorized parties stayed out. Before each race, horses scheduled to run were brought to the barn and examined by Hoop, the official veterinarian, prior to going to post. If any horse looked unfit to run, Hoop scratched him from the field and placed him on the Veterinarian's List, which, according to the California Horse Racing Board, was not "a punitive device but a protection for the racing public, for the physical health of the horses, for the jockeys who ride those horses, for the continuity of racing programs, and for the investment of racing owners." A horse on the vet's list couldn't start again until he'd recovered from his infirmity.

In addition, Hoop was responsible for overseeing the elaborate post-race testing procedure. An assistant took a urine specimen from every winning horse, from the second finisher in exacta races, from the first three horses in stakes races, and from any horse who showed the sort of form reversal that might indicate tampering, as well as occasional random samples. The specimens were flown to Truesdail Labs in Los Angeles, where they were subjected to analysis by gas and thin-layer chromatography, ultraviolet, infrared, and mass spectrometry, and crystalline and color-reaction reagents. The tests were done either singly or in combination and were supposed to reveal any foreign substance present in a horse's system. A positive finding of a so-called prohibited drug set in motion a criminal investigation conducted by the Board. Violators could be charged with felonies and imprisoned. Penalties for the abuse of permitted medications were not so harsh, although recidivists were sometimes suspended or stripped of their licenses.

When I went to visit Hoop, Ruling Don's breakdown was still on my mind. I had come to believe that of the official reasons given for placing a horse on the vet's list, only two really had any impact at Golden Gate, the last two, those that protected owners and the Tanforan Association. It seemed to me that a subtle balance had gone awry, that the track was grinding up horses for profit, cannibalizing its own best interests. I thought that horses, and the jockeys who toppled with them when they broke down under unwarranted stress, deserved better.

Hoop thought I was overstating the case. He agreed that California drug laws were broadly written but believed that the penalties for violating them were severe enough to frighten off most would-be offenders. All medications used at California tracks were classified either as prohibited or permitted. Prohibited drugs were more tightly controlled—they had a more immediate and telling effect on performance—and included stimulants, depressants, narcotics, and local anesthetics. Horses being treated with them couldn't race within sixty hours of their last dosage. Phenylbutazone, on the other hand, was permitted and occupied the same catch-all category as steroids, aspirin, muscle relaxants, furosemide (Lasix, a diuretic given to horses who bled from the nostrils under exertion), vitamins, analgesics, and other medications linked less directly to performance. Bute had to be given steadily, not in an arbitrary, on-off, on-off fashion, and it couldn't be given at all on a race day. If it was, said Hoop, it would be detected at the official racing laboratory in Truesdale. Since the start of Tanforan only one infraction had been detected, when excessive levels of bute were found in Moonlight Cocktail's urine after she'd won her race. The stewards decided the extra dose had been given accidentally and fined Steve Gardell, the trainer, two hundred fifty dollars, less than his share of the purse.

"This whole bute thing is blown way out of proportion," Hoop said in annoyance. "It's nothing special. It doesn't make a horse run any faster."

"Doesn't a horse run faster when he's not feeling any pain?"

Hoop adopted a more vigorous tone. "It *doesn't* make a horse run any faster. That's all there is to it. Bute reduces inflammation, nothing further. It's just that everybody's prescribing it now. These fads happen all the time. Once, down at Hollywood Park, the rumor got around that Bobby Frankel was only using three nails in his horseshoes. Frankel's a successful trainer, so the next thing you know everybody's using just three nails." Hoop smiled. "Didn't help, though."

The California Horse Racing Board refused to supply bettors with any information about drugs. I asked Hoop why.

"The drug list is confidential," he said. "We believe certain things shouldn't be made public."

I asked again.

"It's our policy."

This seemed unfair to the fans. Certainly a chronically sore horse running on bute for the first time would show an improvement, and California bettors should be made aware of such things. Some eastern tracks gave drug specifics right on the program, along with scratches and equipment changes.

But what bothered me most in talking to Hoop was his apparent trust in technology. This was the modern romantic affliction, I thought. Nose cones were replacing gushing cataracts as objects of admiration; soon motel walls would be decorated with canvases depicting astronauts blown about like Michelin men in the starry recesses of space. Clearly, the development of new drugs—whether they were anti-inflammatory, analgesics, depressants, or stimulants—would always be a step ahead of the scientific testing procedures necessary to detect them. There was a logical flaw in the Truesdale scheme as well, in that the tests were skewed toward finding doped *winners,* when in fact many a race was fixed by inhibiting a few key horses. Moreover, it was extremely difficult to pin a drug-related crime on an owner or trainer, even with a positive test in hand. Excuses were manifold, ready-made. Maybe a groom who didn't understand English very well mixed up the medications, or maybe he was acting in consort with some other trainer, or on his own, or as an agent for a syndicate, or as part of the Grooms' Liberation Front, and maybe he was gone now—certainly he did it!—lost in the palm-thick jungles of Guatemala. The defense could rest and most likely get off with a fine for negligence. It was a bad idea to turn over your responsibility to machines housed in a plant five hundred miles away.

After an hour I realized that Hoop and I were talking at cross-purposes. His job, as he saw it, wasn't to scratch every sore animal who came into the receiving barn, but to keep a steady procession (ninety-two to a hundred head a day) of what he called "raceably sound" horses moving toward the starting gate. Again it came down to a question of language, of definition. I think I would've defined "raceably sound" far more stringently than Hoop. It wasn't that Hoop was a bad man or even a negligent one. He was only a man of his times, it seemed to me, loyal to what Chief Justice Marshall had defined in 1809 as "that invisible, intangible and artificial being, that mere legal entity," the corporation.

Hoop invited me to stay around and watch him give a pre-race examination. We left the office and I saw grooms leading horses through the arched doorway and around the barn. They wore strained expressions and were on their best behavior. Nearby a man in gray khakis leaned on a push broom and yawned. He was the manure-sweeper. "Not a very interesting job," he said, "but it keeps you busy." Hoop told me he'd be looking for wet bandages, welts, bumps, and other signs of tampering, as well as noticeable lameness. At a signal from him the grooms took their horses into the stalls. He moved to the center of the floor, gave another signal, and watched as the horses came out of the stalls and were led around him. They moved like spokes, and Hoop studied them, concentrating on their legs and scratching his chin with a program. He didn't touch any of them or alter in any way the distance he'd established at the start. After two minutes' observation, he sent the horses to post. They were in the hands of the Racing Vet now, and it was up to him to scratch any animals *he* thought were too lame to run. But he was a Tanforan employee, and the association hated last-minute scratches—they fouled up the bookkeeping, necessitated refunds, and reduced the handle—so it was safe to assume that Hoop's assessment would not be undercut.

VI

I had always imagined the great Florentine horse race, the *palio* of St. John the Baptist, held yearly on June 24 and named in honor of the prize bestowed on the winner, a piece of crimson fabric trimmed with fur, silk, and gold worth three hundred florins, as a majestic event, a ringing forth of bells and horses. The *corso* began at the outskirts of Florence and wound through the streets, stitching together the various districts—Dragon, Golden Lion, Shell, Viper, Unicorn, and so on—into a briefly harmonious whole. After the midday feast spectators drifted out of their houses and took up positions all along the racecourse. Women wore their jewels—pearls, emeralds, rubies—and long embroidered gowns, and men their crushed-velvet caps and capes fringed with mink or ermine. Bright banners hung from windows, and flowers were scattered on the cobbles. The horses were assembled at the Porta al Prato. Their tack consisted of a single lightweight bridle. The jockeys, dressed in white caps and tights and blousy shirts in diverse colors, rode bareback, digging in their heels, and because of this they were respected more for courage than for skill. When the bells of the Palazzo Vecchio rang three times, the horses were released in a pack. Boys climbed the Palazzo's *campanile* and flashed signs to the crowd below, calling the race. At the finish line a group of magistrates sat like stewards, waiting to name the winner, while around them the city lost itself in pageantry and the echo of hoofs on stones.

But in my reading I'd learned other things about the *palio,* how brutal, ugly, and corrupt it could be. Hard-paved streets were tough on horses' legs, and there were so many obstacles along the *corso*—dogs, cats, chickens, children, drunks—that horses often tripped or went off stride, breaking down. One contemporary painting showed a fine white horse spread-eagled on the cobbles, his two front legs bent back and his jockey thrown forward and sprawled across his neck. Riders, too, were expendable. They were constantly getting caught in a pinch or pushed against a wall and thrown or trampled. In some races they carried clubs to use on one another in the pack. Incompetence and limited tack kept sending them off on side trips into the crowd, where they crashed and were spilled again. This happened so often that the Council of Siena once passed an ordinance absolving jockeys of any responsibility for killing or wounding spectators during a race. Sometimes a *palio* was inverted and run as a parodic contest, featuring the most flea-bitten nags available. Then the body count soared. Florentines loved to gamble, and as the amount of money bet on races increased, fixers appeared on the scene, making their usual time-honored arrangements.

VII

After Clarence Pementel picked up Ruling Don's body he hauled it to the San Jose Tallow Works. Pementel had been collecting dead horses for fifty years, as his father had done before him, and he would make this round trip, from his ranch to Golden Gate to San Jose and home again, many times during the course of a racing season. At the tallow works, Ruling Don's hide was stripped and his flesh and bones were ground into a meal that would be sold as poultry feed. A small amount of tallow was rendered from his carcass, and it would later be exported to India or Egypt or Korea or some other country where tallow was still used in the manufacture of soap. The bottom had dropped out of the domestic tallow market when the detergent companies switched over to cheaper substances like coconut oil. Business was so slow at the tallow works that customers had to pay to have their dead stock processed. As for Pementel, he was paid by the track.

VIII

I wanted to forget about Ruling Don but his breakdown kept coming back to me, relentlessly, the sight of him balanced on a stump of bone and the formidable sense of helplessness and betrayal I felt while watching him stumble around. Of course there was no single place to fix the blame. Drug abuse, inadequate supervision of stock, demands of trainers and owners to make a buck, of racing associations to make a bigger buck, the industry's inability to police itself, the pressures of year-round racing, the choice of expediency over nurturance, quantity over quality, I could name twenty-five other contributory factors off the top of my head, but in the end they added up not to an answer but to a familiar syndrome, libraries closing, rivers dammed, condominiums going up, all in the cold blue glow of flickering tubes.

IX

Some months after Laudomia Strozzi of Ferrara rejected him as a suitor, Girolamo Savonarola, then twenty-two, awoke in the night to cascades of freezing water spilling onto his head. This *acqua frigidissima* was only part of a dream, but it had a cleansing effect anyway, dousing the carnal fires that had been troubling Savonarola since adolescence. A short time later he entered the Convent of San Domenico in Bologna and dedicated his life to a vision of spiritual purity, the soul liberated from tormented flesh. When he came to power in Florence following Lorenzo's death, he offered up his vision to mourning citizens. An Antichrist would soon appear, he said, but the city would hold fast against the onslaught and be transformed into a new Jerusalem that would serve as a Christian exemplar for all the peoples on earth. Florence would become an Ark of the spirit, with a government enlightened by personal sacrifice and the grace of God. Savonarola's audience was receptive, and his vision was embraced. "Courtesans and gamblers went into hiding," wrote the historian Ferdinand Shevill, "ribald street songs were replaced by pious hymns; men and women alike adopted a plain and modest dress and were untiring in their attendance at mass and sermon." Botticelli surrendered to the spirit, and so, too, did Pico, while more skeptical Humanists retreated more deeply into an idealized past, forsaking the present entirely.

But the politicians in Florence allowed Savonarola his freedom only so long as he stayed outside their sphere of influence. The minute his constituency pushed him to the fore, his days were numbered. Soon he was caught up in political intrigue and locked into a power struggle with the Pope, Alexander Borgia, a lusty corrupt robber baron who'd bought the papacy and was eagerly making it pay. Savonarola advocated Florentine support of Charles VIII of France, whom he considered the instrument of God, a leading general in the army of reformation, while Alexander, embarrassed earlier by Charles's forces, had already thrown his support to the anti-French league (Venice, Naples, Milan) and wanted the Arno government to enlist on his side as added protection against future French incursions. In the next few years Alexander waged subtle and not-so-subtle war against the friar, challenging his authority, excommunicating him, and when his support dwindled at last, charging him with heresy. Savonarola was found guilty by two church commissioners, and on May 23, 1498, a gallows was erected in the Piazza della Signoria. Beneath it wood and brush was arranged in a pyre. Along with two other Dominicans, Savonarola was hanged, then burned. Scavengers collected his ashes and threw them into the Arno, to be carried out to sea.

In 1522 the first of a series of plagues struck Florence. By 1530 the city was blockaded and food was scarce. Ass-meat was a delicacy, all the cats around had been eaten, and people spent hours hunting the countryside for swallows, owls, falcons, anything with meat on its bones. An egg cost ten *soldi*, a rat thirteen. Among Florentines in need of explanations it was said that the plague was not of local origin, but had been brought in by a stranger from Rome.

X

From the curved windows of Clifford Goodrich's office I could see the track and the Albany hills, and in the other direction, looking south, the Bay and San Francisco. This was the executive suite, with plush carpeting, a new desk, comfortable furniture, a bathroom, and to the rear of the suite a darkened nook where the directors of the Tanforan and Pacific Racing associations sometimes held their meetings. None of them were seated around the table now, but in the silence that money buys I could feel the power of their connections, the interlocking of stocks and bonds: *Director, Hyatt Corporation of America; Partner, J. Barth & Co.; Director, State Savings & Loan; President, British Motor Car Distributors, Ltd.; President, Zel-*

lerbach Paper Company; Director, First Western Bank & Trust; Member, Commonwealth Club. These connections, inherited, married into, purchased, bartered for, occasionally earned, were more important than the directors' names, fixing them more firmly in time and space. They seldom visited the track anyway, unless a horse they owned was running or an "occasion" like the California Derby appeared in the pages of their social calendars. On these days they traipsed past the press box heading for the executive suite, for the big picture and the comfort of a 270° view, dragging hangers-on behind them and smoking big cigars.

Goodrich, general manager of both Pacific and Tanforan, was the directors' man on the spot. The job was a tricky one for anybody who retained, as Goodrich seemed to, a respect for honesty. He was intelligent, reasonably direct, and still young enough, at thirty-five, to look ill at ease when he had to skirt around the edges of a potentially incriminating question. In college he'd been an ace pitcher—physically, he resembled Don Drysdale, with the same rangy southern California quality to his frame—but he had suffered an arm injury and, instead of signing a contract, had gone to work at Santa Anita after graduation. He'd worked there since summer vacations in high school, starting at the turnstiles, and at six or seven other tracks before settling in as general manager at Golden Gate in 1977. Presently Goodrich was having a rough time of it. Figures showed that attendance at Pacific's winter meeting was down 8.1 percent, with a concomitant drop in the handle, and early returns at Tanforan gave no indication of reversing the trend. So Goodrich found himself in a bind, caught between running a racetrack properly, as he'd learned to do from the ground up, and hedging in order to satisfy the directors' and other investors' dissatisfaction about decreasing profits.

When a group of Bay Area businessmen bought Golden Gate

Fields in 1965 and formed a holding company (Bay Area Turf Club, later Bay Area Sports Enterprises) to disperse stock in the Pacific and Tanforan Associations, the future of racing in California seemed illimitable. In its first year of control the group pumped a million dollars into the decrepit plant (the only major overhaul they would make in fifteen years, except for the addition of a turf course in 1972), then sat back and raked in the profits. "The combination of an illustrious history and progressive new management has brought an exciting spirit of Renaissance to Bay Area racing," the company flack wrote in a vintage press release. "Last year attendance at Golden Gate Fields was up eleven percent to lead major racecourses in this regard." In 1966 Bay Area Turf Club stock split ten-for-one, and the corporation declared a five-dollar-per-share dividend on the new over-the-counter issue, which had a par value of a hundred dollars.

About the same time, the California Horse Racing Board hired the Stanford Research Institute in Palo Alto to assess the overall economic condition of the racing industry in the state. The results of the SRI study, Project I-5329, are instructive. In order for the industry to continue to grow, said the report, it had to attract more members of the occupational and educational elite, as well as young adults with money to burn. Two factors currently kept such people away: The word *racing* had negative connotations for them, and the sport's complexity, its terminology and arcana, put them off. SRI suggested that associations educate the market, clean up racing's image, and simplify procedures as much as possible. In a subsection, "Other Market Findings Significant for the Formulation of Public Policy," the report cited several business practices that might imperil the industry's future. Racing associations, for instance, were not plowing enough money back into their tracks. Instead they chose to pay big dividends, double the going rate in similarly structured nonfinancial corporations. In some holding companies, curious accounting methods obtained—tax write-offs for depreciation were very high, while those for fixed plant and equipment costs were very low. Furthermore, fans were complaining about the quality of stock allowed to compete at racetracks. People wanted to see better horses, but associations were doing little to cater to this desire. "Horse quality," said the report, "was found to be of critical importance for developing and maintaining widespread interest in horse racing. Improvement in the current quality of horses running at California race meetings would be likely to have more effect in increasing attendance in northern as compared with southern California." The state's breeding industry, "with a critical shortage of high-quality stallions," was also in need of support, and again racing associations had been for the most part unwilling to help. The report's final criticism was telling: Profits made by racing associations were too high, and purses these same associations paid to horsemen were too low.

At Golden Gate a few efforts were made to educate the public —Saturday morning open house, more free handicapping information—but in general the SRI report, particularly its insistence on the necessity of upgrading the quality of stock performing, was largely ignored. Instead, racing associations attempted to increase their already inflated profit margins by requesting the right to run even more races per season. From 1967 to 1978 the number of racing days in California jumped from 633 to 996 a year. Where the horses for this expansion came from is anybody's guess; why they needed to be medicated before running is not.

When I mentioned the SRI report to Goodrich, he refused to credit its arguments. The associations weren't to blame, he said. Competition from other sports (basketball, two baseball teams, soccer, hockey, harness and quarter-horse racing) had reduced significantly the potential Bay Area audience for thoroughbreds, but the state of California was the real villain. At California tracks in 1978, eighty-three percent of the money wagered was returned to the public via winning payoffs, while the other seventeen percent, known as the take-out, was divided among racing associations, horsemen, and the state. Over the last ten years, the state had been gradually appropriating a larger and larger share, $109 million, or forty-three percent, in 1977, which left the other partners short in the pocket. The substantial profits of the past had been whittled down to slivers (unions had helped with the whittling, Goodrich said), and associations were being "forced" to pass along escalating costs to the fans.

Recently the California Horse Racing Board had decided to sponsor another study, to be undertaken not by SRI but by Temple, Barker & Sloane, Inc., of Lexington, Massachusetts, and Goodrich hoped that when it was completed, it would give the associations some statistical support for their lobbying efforts in Sacramento. He gave me a copy of the management summary of the new report as soon as it reached his desk. Indeed, "An Analysis of the California Horse Racing Industry" made a strong case against the state's inequitable allocation of the take-out and proposed a model for redistribution, but it also reiterated many of the criticisms in the SRI report.

> Attendance declines are the result of many factors. Consumer research points to the quality of the racing, the quality of the facilities, the level of the take-out and the appearance or perception of race manipulation as factors that influence attendance.

So in the end the directors' complaints had about as much poignancy as a spoiled child's on his first awareness of limits.

What I was witnessing at Golden Gate was the penultimate act of a karmic melodrama, the chickens coming home to roost. I asked Goodrich what he planned to do.

"We're going to start lobbying more heavily," he said. "We've got to get some legislative relief."

What about the stock running?

"I don't know too much about it," Goodrich said.

XI

Cardinal Ippolito d'Este once commissioned Benvenuto Cellini to create for him a saltcellar more imaginative and elaborate than any saltcellar ever made before. He gave the sculptor two designs and asked him to choose between them, but Cellini, who was known for his pride, scrapped both and submitted instead a model so ambitious in conception that the cardinal balked. A friend told him the design was too complex to be executed, and the Este prelate withdrew his commission. Cellini, angered, swore that the cardinal would live to see the saltcellar completed "a hundred times more richly." He was right. The finished object, of gold, studded with gemstones, depicted Neptune, triton in hand, guarding salt, and opposite him the figure of Earth, female and recumbent, guarding pepper. Other figures representing dawn and day, twilight and night, and the seasons were carved in bas-relief around the base. Looking at the photograph again, I was impressed by Cellini's skill and audacity, but I thought at the same time he'd outstripped the object's purpose and gone beyond it into decadence.

XII

In the evening I took a walk on the backstretch and ended up at Pichi's stall. Nobody was around, not even Bo, and I was

most conscious of the sound of animals, Bud Keen's goat braying, dumb little Urashima Taro pawing, Dantero picking at his
feed tub with his teeth. Pichi just stood there looking at me,
immobile, showing neither affection nor distaste, and I listened
to the slight sibilance of her breathing and studied the white
blaze between her eyes. She stood there calm as salt, beating
like a pulse.

Chapter Nine

In 1475 Francesca Buonarroti, who was pregnant, went riding in Caprese and fell from her horse. Her husband, Ludovico, was afraid she might lose the child she was carrying, but the townspeople assured him that the fall was instead a good omen. Shortly thereafter a son, named Michelangelo, was born.

II

All horses are descended from the so-called dawn horse, whose fossil remains were discovered in 1838 near Suffolk, England, and subsequently dated to the Lower Eocene epoch some seventy million years ago. Because the skeleton was small, measuring less than twenty inches high at the shoulder, scientists grouped it mistakenly among the ratlike hyraxes and named it *Hyracotherium*. By the time similar finds were made in northern Europe and the upper Mississippi Valley, Darwinian theory had gained a purchase in scientific circles, and the fossils in question were reclassified as relatives of the present-day horse. Charles Marsh of Yale contributed a new taxonomic label, *Eohippus*.

Out of this little fox-sized animal the modern thoroughbred evolved.

The evolutionary path was convoluted, though, winding intricately through several species before arriving at the modern horse's true progenitor, *Equus caballus*. There was *Mesohippus*, the first horse adapted to grazing; *Parahippus*, about three inches taller and bearing stripes on its coat; *Merychippus*, whose humped withers and dentition provided another advance; and *Pliohippus*, taller still, with more delicate legs and toeless feet. *Equus caballus* flourished during the Pleistocene age; the animal was about fifty-two inches high at the withers, strongly built, and of a hardy constitution. The great Pleistocene floods wiped out the species in the Americas, but it survived throughout Europe and Asia. One herd disappeared into the Mongolian wilderness and was not discovered until the last century, when the Russian explorer who found the herd lent it his name: *Equus przewalskii*.

By 4000 B.C. the first horses had been domesticated and were used for pulling carts. In Greece, circa 1700 B.C., the carts metamorphosed into the famous two-horse chariots of *Ben Hur*. Though these chariots were primarily instruments of war, Greeks did race them on occasion and bred special horses in the Peloponnesus to pull them. Columbus reintroduced horses to North America on his second voyage in 1493, leaving behind some representative Andalusian stock in the West Indies. Horses soon became part of the cargo on almost every ship bound for the New World, and Amerindian tribes in Texas and New Mexico were quick to latch on to as many of them as they could. Apaches and Comanches raided Spanish encampments and traded stolen horses to more northerly tribes, as did French and Spanish traders (though less flamboyantly), and by 1730 even the Yakima in Washington owned stock.

The lightest, fastest, and in many ways finest descendants of *Eohippus* were by then to be found in North Africa. Two closely related types, the Arab and the Barb (for Barbary Coast, now Libya), had been inbred meticulously over centuries to maintain their purity and prepotency, that all-important ability to transmit signal characteristics to an offspring (called, in breeding terminology, *stamping the get*). In Africa the cult of noble blood was born. Never be hard on a fine horse, the Arabs said, for his nature will cause him to rebel. At night, out on the desert sands, the Arabs brought prized mounts into their tents and treated them like members of the family. Then there is the Saharan legend of the original horse breeder, Ishmael. A mare of Ishmael's gave birth to a filly who was too weak to keep up with the caravan, but rather than destroy the foal—her blood was noble—Ishmael ordered his men to wrap her in goatskin and carry her along. This saved her life but crippled her legs. She became known as the Crooked One, but in spite of her deformity she achieved high honor as the taproot, or base, mare for an excellent line of females, the *Benat el-A'waj,* Daughters of the Crooked One, who in turn became the *Kehila.* In Arabic *Kehila* means *purely* or *thoroughly* bred.

By the early sixteenth century horses were in short supply in England because so much stock had been lost during the War of the Roses. Henry VIII, a sportsman dependent on horses for hunting and tournaments, took measures to improve the situation. Primarily, he relied on neighboring countries for imports, which complemented an edict of his predecessor, Henry VII, who in 1496 had banned the export of stock from Britain. The accent was on speed and lightness, and away from the qualities embodied by a prior favorite, the great horse, a big strong animal bred for combat and capable of transporting a man-at-arms and sixty pounds of armor into a fray. Francesco Gonzaga,

Marchese di Mantova, sent Henry broodmares and Barb stallions. Ferdinand of Aragon contributed two Spanish horses worth a thousand ducats; the gesture was so grand it caused speculation about Ferdinand's sanity. Over the years more and more Arabs and Barbs found their way into the king's stables at Greenwich. The Master of the Horse interbred them, and the offspring were raced in gentlemanly contests against horses from the stables of Henry's friends and acquaintances. Gradually this racing fever spread to the populace. When municipal racecourses like those at Chester, Newmarket, and Croyden opened, the demand for animals bred exclusively to race increased.

The problem of breeding such a horse fell to the wealthy and their studmasters. No real breakthrough occurred until by luck three exceptionally prepotent stallions arrived in Britain within a forty-year period. In 1688 Captain Byerley captured at the siege of Vienna a handsome "Turk"—actually an Arab courser who'd been bought or stolen by the Turkish officer riding him— and brought him home; in 1704 Richard Darley purchased from Syrian friends in Aleppo a four-year-old Arabian and sent him to his brother in Yorkshire; and in 1730 the second earl of Godolphin acquired from Edward Coke of Derbyshire an Arabian who'd been foaled in Yemen and had once purportedly belonged to the King of France. From the get of these stallions, the three great thoroughbred bloodlines were created. Characteristics of the Godolphin Arabian were disseminated by Matchem (foaled in 1748) and those of the Byerley Turk by Herod (foaled in 1758). But the most important line proceeds from the Darley Arabian's relative Eclipse, born in 1764, the year of the great eclipse of the sun. Eclipse was a champion who won all his races without ever being whipped, spurred, or headed, and when he went to stud in 1771 he rode to the stables in a cart, so precious had he become. The moment was a triumphant one for *E. caballus,* reversing as it did the earliest images of domestication. The horse was in ascendance, fully pedigreed, the subject of oil paintings that hung above mantelpieces in the parlors of princes and magnates, captivating them just as its ancestors had captivated the cave dwellers at Lascaux.

This, then, was the thoroughbred, an offshoot of human longing, a particle of nature molded to fit within a construct, derived from Arabian stock tainted only slightly in couplings with royal mares and a few mares of mysterious and perhaps humble origins. But the progress from concept to flesh was not so orderly as some track historians make it sound. Breeding went on all over Britain, without much supervision or control, and the genealogical records of sires and broodmares were often confused or faked and sometimes unavailable. Names of horses were changed frequently, almost always when ownership changed, and were abbreviated or misspelled or otherwise fudged—Matchem was actually Match 'Em, and Herod more rightly *King* Herod. Occasionally the same name was bestowed on two or three animals in succession, father and son, mother and daughter. The terms Barb, Arab, and Turk were used interchangeably, and not every mare billed as "royal" came in fact from the king's stables. John Cheney, editor of *An Historical List of all Horse-Matches Run, And of all Plates and Prizes Run for in England in 1727,* the first known attempt at a stud book (a record of stallions' bloodlines and performances on the track), couldn't vouch for the accuracy of the pedigrees he included. A later competitor named Heber confessed in the preface to his *Calendar* that mistakes were unavoidable when cataloging genealogical data. Despite these complications the thoroughbred, simply by having been brought into existence, posed a new problem, that of refinement. How could breeders improve a horse's speed and stamina? They started with blood.

III

The blood of thoroughbreds is thick and hot, with more hemoglobin and red cells and a higher cell density than are found in ordinary horses, but it isn't the medium in which characteristics like speed and stamina are suspended or by which they're transmitted to offspring. Breeders in the days before Mendel thought it was. For them blood held the resonances of generations, all the secrets, and they were engaged in a perpetual search for a master formula to guide them in their tinkering. Their approach was alchemical. How do you extract the gold of a perfect racehorse from the base substances of sire and dam? What are the correct proportions? How much sprinter in the mix, how much router, and from which family? Darley Arabian's? Byerley Turk's?

Some breeders believed in telegony. In telegonic theory, a pregnant mare received infusions of the stallion's blood from her developing fetus, through "channels as yet unknown to Science," and retained even after foaling a few of the sire's precious traits. She could then pass them along to subsequent foals even if they were the get of a different stallion. Her blood became twice-prized, hermaphroditic, offering breeders a double hit of male potency, a second set of masculine characteristics for the price of one. Colonel Vuillers's dosage system was somewhat more sophisticated, but equally useless. Vuillers attempted to concoct a recipe for mixing blood in perfect ratio. He traced the history of each horse listed in the stud book of his day back through twelve generations, recording its four thousand ancestors. Patterns began to emerge, certain horses showing up time and again in the lineage of champions. Counting each ancestor as a unit of blood, Vuillers could then specify the right mix for, say, a speedy filly: combine 288 parts Birdcatch, 351 parts Touchstone, 186 parts Voltaire . . .

Mendelian genetics brought to a close the era of corpuscular mysticism, but breeders continued to look for a definitive way to predict the outcome of pairings. Though broodmares were known to be more effective than stallions at passing along their characteristics, most systems concentrated on studs and their ability to stamp their get. An exception was the Bruce Lowe system, which still has currency today. Lowe, an Englishman, examined the pedigrees of the winners of three major English classics, the Derby, Oaks, and St. Leger, and traced them back in *female* line to their earliest known ancestors, as recorded in volume one of the stud book. The descendants of Tregonwell's Natural Barb Mare had won most often, so Lowe ranked this family first in importance. The descendants of Burton's Barb Mare were second-best at producing winners and became Bruce Lowe Family Number Two. In all Lowe ranked forty-three families. While his work was useful, pointing out the strengths and weaknesses of several lines, it was attacked immediately in the States. Americans protested the inherent bias against United States–born or –bred mares (their foals seldom competed in European classics even if they were outstanding racehorses), and other breeders with mares who'd been slighted criticized Lowe for devising a system bound to perpetuate itself. His "prophecy" was self-fulfilling. Top-ranked mares would be bred to top-ranked stallions and naturally produce superior foals. Later on, experts poked holes in Lowe's research, but Lowe still has defenders in breeding circles, perhaps because he chose to focus on feminine principles in a world skewed radically toward the masculine.

Other breeding techniques have gone in and out of vogue as their results have been demonstrated on the track. Inbreeding, the practice of mating two closely related horses, maintains genetic purity and intensifies familial characteristics, both positive and negative, to varying degrees. A sire and a dam who share great speed and a nasty disposition may well yield a comet-like colt, but the colt might also be too troublesome to handle. Sometimes two families show an affinity for one another, called a nick, and breeding between family members produces excellent foals. But nicks are not infallible. The energy around them always dissipates, often in a single generation, and inferior specimens begin to issue. In the end there are no shortcuts, no formulas that have infallibly proven their worth over an extended period. When you talk to breeders they speak of simple commonsense principles. Use quality stock, they say. Learn your bloodlines. Watch for peculiarities. Does a stallion transmit more of his characteristics to his fillies than to his colts? Then he's a broodmare-sire. Cover your mares with stallions who'll complement them, supplying talents they lack, or try breeding speed to speed or stamina to stamina in hopes that the desired characteristic will be emboldened. There's not much else you can do, they mutter, moving dirt around with a boot tip, feeling handicapped because another force is at work and they can't quite get to it, something beyond eugenics, the crackling around the bodies of lovers bent on conceiving, heat lightning, what the mystic says in saying nothing: a hole in the smoke. Every now and then a breeder makes contact with this energy, harnessing it briefly, but only one person ever tried to describe it. That was Federico Tesio, the Wizard of Dormello.

IV

"My aim," wrote Tesio, "was to breed and raise a race-horse which, over any distance, could carry the heaviest weight in the shortest time." Tesio was mad about horses. In his youth he rode as a steeplechase jockey in England and traveled to Argentina to break broncos on the pampas and then drove deeper into

South America and led a caravan consisting of two natives, thirty-nine stallions, and a mare on an exploratory tour of Patagonia, from Rio Negro to Punta Arenas, over an endless stretch of prairie, shooting llamas and ostriches for food and hobnobbing with the caciques of wandering Indian tribes. One evening the caravan drew to a halt near a red hillock that supposedly marked an oasis, but the spring was almost dry. The horses went without water, but during the night they broke away from camp and returned to a spring they'd left the day` before, covering thirty miles in the dark by the shortest possible route. How did they do it? They have a sixth sense, Tesio said, and this was their real attraction, this extrasensory quality. In horses, Tesio found an outlet for his weirdest speculations about the workings of the cosmos. He was a student of energy, its distribution and transmission, how it affected the will, what happened when it dwindled, and he believed in wildness and passion and the supreme power of sexual magnetism to affect the makeup and destiny of offspring.

In 1898 Tesio retired from his life of action and started a breeding farm near Lake Maggiore in northern Italy for the ostensible purpose of studying heredity. He chose thoroughbreds as the medium for his research because he loved them and because their histories were recorded in such detail. At Dormello he compiled a magnificent library of arcana. Ancient stud books; descriptions of races; thoroughbred biographies (Flying Childers, by Darley Arabian out of Betty Leeds: "In his earlier years he used to carry the mail bags between Hull and Doncaster and on the road he was unbeaten"); descriptions of their markings and temperaments; texts on biochemistry, genetics, and electronics; accounts of odd experiments, like those of Professor Morro with his ergograph, a machine which measured fatigue by graphing the curve of exhaustion (a pulley was attached to the subject's middle finger)—all these materials came to rest on Tesio's shelves and provided him with evidence for his fringiest bouts of speculation.

He expected his farm to be an immediate success, but it faltered at first ("I had not yet learned to reflect . . .") and he couldn't compete with other Italian breeders. Then in 1906 something miraculous happened to him on a train going from Pisa to Rome. (Miraculous things were always happening to Tesio.) He discovered the existence of hybrids. Another passenger, a foreigner, was reading a booklet entitled "Mendelism," and Tesio snatched it up when the foreigner stepped out into the aisle. The booklet told of Mendel's work with sweet peas, how he'd crossed tall and dwarf strains to produce hybrids and how after several experiments he'd been able to predict the results of subsequent crossings. This came as a revelation to Tesio. It had never occurred to him before that thoroughbreds weren't all *di puro sangue,* purebred. Now he knew why two foals, full brothers, of the same sire and dam, could turn out so different, the one chestnut-colored and a great runner, the other bay and mediocre. If he could learn how Mendel's laws operated among thoroughbreds, he would have the key to creating an ultimate racehorse.

Here began Tesio's Mendelian misadventure. He confined his inquiry to a single inherited characteristic, coat color. Before making any crosses he needed to determine how many true colors there were and how frequently each had appeared over the last two centuries. The research involved was mind-boggling, but Tesio was aided by the tabulations of others, particularly the German Herman Goos, and in less than a year he had cataloged the coat color of every thoroughbred whose birth had been recorded. The statistics convinced him that only two true colors existed: bay, the darker, and chestnut, the fairer. He dismissed gray and the special red of roans as "diseases," relatively uncommon aberrations that issued in violation of Mendel's laws. Chestnuts (Ch), he said, were always purebred—whenever two chestnuts mated they always produced another chestnut—but bays could be either purebred (Pbb) or hybrid (Hbb), and the three varieties could be crossed in six different ways.

Pbb + Pbb = Pbb
Ch + Ch = Ch
Pbb + Ch = Hbb
Pbb + Hbb = Hbb
Ch + Hbb = Ch or Hbb
Hbb + Hbb = Pbb or Ch or Hbb #1 or Hbb #2

Next he tried to discern which color was dominant. A check of horses entered at major English racetracks in a randomly selected year showed bays predominating four to one. Tesio wondered why. He knew that color was pigment, and pigment was a chemical compound, but these facts were worthless until he heard about the experiments of his friend Paul Fournier. When Fournier had inserted a strand of bay hair into a high-frequency solenoid, a cylindrical conductor of electricity, it gave off a red spark. A strand of chestnut hair gave off a yellow spark. In the spectrum, red has a greater wavelength than yellow and therefore, said Tesio, leaping, bay horses must have a greater wavelength than chestnut horses. This explained their predominance, for in nature "the small gives way to the large."

At last Tesio was ready to apply what he'd learned. But the data he'd gathered puzzled him and he didn't know how to proceed. One day, though, he recalled an "Oriental" tale from Arabia that gave him a clue.

An old man and a boy, riding on a camel, were fleeing across the desert pursued by a group of Bedouins with murderous intent. When the camel began to show signs of tiring, the old man said to the boy, who was clinging to his waist: "Look back and tell me the color of the leading horse."

"It is a chestnut," answered the boy.

"The chestnut is fast, but he will soon tire," said the old man, and they continued their flight.

After a while he repeated his question and the boy replied: "Now a gray horse is in front."

"Never fear, he too will tire," said the old man hopefully, and on they fled.

A little later, when the camel showed further signs of fatigue, the old man again repeated the question. •

"Now a bay horse has taken the lead," answered the boy.

"In that case," sighed the old man, "let us commit our souls to Allah."

Tesio inferred from the story that a chestnut coat meant speed and a bay coat meant staying power. Since he could breed bays and chestnuts at will, he seemed about to triumph. By carefully selecting his stock and controlling matings he could, with mathematical certainty, produce the ultimate racehorse. All that was left to do was to verify the final element, the correlation of speed to coat color. Again he turned to racing history and tabulated the winners of five English classics over the last century and found, to his utter despair, that the tale had misled him: there was *absolutely no correlation* between coat color and speed or staying power or winning ability or anything else under the sun. Tesio was appalled. All along he'd been assuming that characteristics were transmitted from parents to offspring in standard combinations, like eggs arranged neatly in a cardboard carton, but now, after years of work, he saw that the opposite was true.

In hybrid animals, even if highly selected, each separate character is passed on independently. Moreover, he decided, speed and stamina were not separate characters but instead the result of other characters in combination. They were nothing more than *tendencies.* So he was stuck.

V

But Tesio had never belonged in a world of figures. His genius, like Pico's, was for registering previously unperceived concordances and applying them to the breeding art. What he saw, he saw in flashes. Several disparate notions would suddenly cohere, and he'd understand that inbreeding was useful not only because it reduced the variables in a pairing, but because the deities of many religions were closely related. The myth of perfection had its roots in proximity. Isis and Osiris conceived Horus, the God of Agriculture, while they were still in their mother's womb, and Jupiter birthed Minerva parthenogenetically, right from his brain. According to the Bible, the entire human race was a by-product of the most severe inbreeding, Adam coupling with his fleshed-out rib. Therefore, inbreeding made sense; divinity provided the supporting testimony.

Tesio was an adept of such equations. Nicks were effective, he said, because their "energic make-up" was the result of the harmonic combination of electromagnetic waves mixing together as pleasantly as oil and vinegar on salad greens. Have you ever noticed, he would ask, how the markings on wild animals (penguins, tigers) always occur symmetrically, identical on both sides of the body, while in thoroughbreds asymmetry always prevails? The stars on a filly's forehead, those little white spots, often have a comet's tail that trails down toward the nose, swerving to one side "as if the brush had slipped from the painter's hand." This was a consequence of hybridism, a disorder caused by man.

Mendelian laws operate randomly, said Tesio, and yet all thoroughbreds have two special traits, "a high degree of nervous energy and a certain 'quality' derived from selection." These traits, he felt, must be transmitted in some manner not accounted for by the laws, passed on directly rather than inherited. Tesio did not know quite how. By "quality" he meant personality, the way a colt or filly favors sire or dam and recapitulates aspects of the behavior of one or the other. Nervous energy was a more inclusive term and stood for willpower, sexual drive, the life-force. Every horse was given a set amount of it at birth, and no more. This was a thoroughbred's capital. Success depended on expenditure, turning on the juice when necessary, but also, and equally, on periods of rest, during which the energy stores were replenished. If a mare had squandered too much of her energy while racing, she wouldn't have enough left to pass on to her foals when she was first bred. Good racing mares were often poor broodmares, at least until they'd been rested for a while, but lightly raced mares and mares who'd never raced at all produced a large percentage of successful distance runners. Stallions who'd raced until the age of six were poor studs, tired and burned out, and the descendants of any horse who'd run on drugs would be low on energy for a generation or two.

Tesio believed that horses had to couple fervidly, almost swooning, to fully charge their get. To illustrate his point, he told the story of Cavaliere Ginistrelli of Naples and his beautiful filly Signorina. Ginistrelli had taken her to England and raced her at Newmarket, where she'd beaten most horses in her class, and he had high hopes for her as a broodmare, but Signorina yielded only mediocre colts despite being covered by premier stallions. In a last-gasp attempt to coax something marvelous out of her, Ginistrelli engaged the services of the great stud Isinglass for three hundred guineas. On the appointed morning Signorina's stable boy led her down High Street toward Isinglass's stall. It was the custom for third-rate studs wanting for business to be showcased on High, paraded up and down like low-rent gigolos, and one of them, Chaleureux (*warm,* in French), caught a whiff of Signorina and became intoxicated. Signorina responded in kind and wouldn't move.

Ginistrelli accepted the romance with equanimity. "They love!" he exclaimed. "A love match it shall be." Eleven months later Signorina gave birth to a daughter, Signoretta, who grew up lovely and swift, a star filly, and went on to win England's Derby and then, two days later, the Oaks, a feat which only two other fillies had ever accomplished. Later, Signorina was bred to Isinglass and bore a half-sister to Signoretta, Star of Naples. Ginistrelli auctioned Star off for five thousand guineas. She raced steadily until her fifth birthday but never finished first.

"The arrows of an equine cupid roused the sexual urge to a maximum of tension," Tesio wrote, disregarding possible Mendelian explanations for the disparity between Signoretta and Star of Naples, "which endowed the resulting individual with exceptional energy." He went on to add that a filly of Signoretta's caliber could never be produced by artificial insemination. Horses brought into existence by means of tubes, needles, and disembodied sperm would of course have no nervous energy. They looked normal, yes, and inherited their traits normally, but they had no drive, no will to win. In the past twenty years no thoroughbred conceived artificially had won a classic race anywhere in the world. Only nature could bestow the muse-kiss, that transcendent infusion.

Then Tesio stated *his* law.

All life is based on the consumption of energy to gain supremacy and on rest to restore that energy. In the rivalry for selection of racing stock, no thoroughbred family can hold the supremacy of success for more than a small number of generations in direct line. This number of generations and the degree of their attainment are irrevocably limited by nature. When these limits are reached, the top producer of the moment must surrender his supremacy to another producer slightly inferior as an individual, who may occasionally belong to a collateral branch but in most instances will represent another family altogether. He in turn will start a new line of top stars. After running its cycle this line too will surrender the sceptre—which it may eventually regain after a period of rest.

VI

A photograph of Tesio as an old man shows him leaning on his cane, watching a race at Ascot. His head, bald and settled like a Brancusi egg inside his fedora, seems too big for his body, as though ideas had made it grow, pushing bone and flesh outward toward the ethereal realm he loved to explore. In the town of Dormello people called him the Wizard. Over the years he bred countless champions, including Nearco, who was undefeated in fourteen outings and just as magnificent at stud, siring Nasrullah, who sired Noor, who beat Citation twice at Golden Gate, signifying a diaspora of no mean proportions, and Ribot, who was small and a little dumpy but who won four European championships as a four-year-old and went on to stand successfully in England, Italy, and the United States. Between 1911 and 1953 Tesio's horses won the Italian Derby twenty times. He sent his mares across the globe in search of seed, following his hunches, exercising infinite care in selection, and yet he would sell any of his stock, even Nearco, if the price was right. Attachment? Tesio had no use for it. There was no question of perfection after all. Every thoroughbred was as close to perfection as it could be.

At Dormello Tesio worked from dawn to dusk. He employed

no trainers or stable managers and supervised everything himself. The farm was divided into several smaller farms, *poderi,* and horses were parceled among them by class, yearling fillies here, broodmares there. If contagious disease struck, Tesio could find its source more readily and keep it from spreading. He wouldn't irrigate any of the pastures because irrigation was *contro natura* and robbed the grass of its strength. In autumn, when the pastures began to wither and turn brown, horses used their hoofs to dig up roots, and extended their necks as far as they could to reach the last green leaves of the acacia trees. They were nervous and wanted to migrate south, said Tesio, just as they'd done before being domesticated. Their sixth sense, which operated like a radio receiver, picked up the distant vibrations of winter and formed in their minds an image of the earth barren and stripped of greenery, of nourishment. So when the leaves fell and the breeze turned cold, Tesio sent his horses to Olgiata, an estate in the Roman Campagna where it was always warm and the grass grew all winter long.

VII

Reading Tesio excited me. He brought me closer to what I was after, confirming suspicions about thoroughbreds I'd held from the very beginning. I thought their attraction was deeply mystical, deriving from some long-standing though lately violated bond between humans and animals, but the traditional view of racing— that it was a gambler's sport dependent on greenbacks for its survival—was at odds with this perception and kept confusing me. Tesio had the opposite effect. He made me more confident in what I believed. Gambling was no doubt central to the racetrack scheme, but the sort of wager being made had a double nature and was of a different order than generally supposed.

Finally the elements were starting to cohere. A fragment of

dialogue, notes scribbled on the back of a program, something I'd observed on the backstretch a month ago—they were all coming together for the first time. It was mid-morning and I should have been doing my handicapping, but I decided not to go to the races that afternoon. Instead I'd follow Tesio's lead and visit a breeding farm. Somebody had told me earlier in the meet about Windsor Thoroughbreds, a modest operation about sixty miles north of Albany, and I bought a six-pack and headed for Sonoma County. I wasn't sure what I'd find there, but the *act* of going felt right; it had the exactitude of one of those magical bets.

Windsor was a country town, small and poor, with a dusty main drag, two blocks of sidewalk, and a slow steady corona of heat rising from the ground. The heat was constant, even in May, and people on the street, farmers, ranchers, migrant workers, withdrew into pockets of shade and stood there in silence, unwilling to move. The men wore straw hats and jeans or overalls, and the women had chubby arms and combed their hair back into tight unflattering buns, which made their faces look as round and crusty as pie fresh from the oven. But outside town the country illusion was punctured by the spindly wooden frames of houses going up in a subdivision. Somewhere paint was already being mixed into the familiar subdivision hues, brown, dark brown, brown-green, and olive drab.

I saw a sign outside a church (TOO LATE! IS WRITTEN ON THE GATES OF HELL) and then the sign for Windsor Thoroughbreds. Country-and-western music played through the screen door of a ramshackle farmhouse, and I had to knock for a long time before John Ryan appeared. Ryan looked as if he'd just gotten up from a nap. He was a tall thin unshaven man in a western shirt and maroon-colored jeans. A safety pin was hooked through a vent hole of his Red Wing baseball cap. Ryan was a rancher and breeder from way back. His grandfather had once owned the largest herd of Black Angus in the nation, three thousand head run on twelve thousand acres near Sioux City, Iowa. Ryan had started with cattle himself but switched over to thoroughbreds about fifteen years ago. He and his wife, Laverne, had been in Windsor for three years. They were managers and part-owners of the ranch, forty gently rounded acres with picturesque fences, barns, and pastures. The place looked ideal for raising horses. Business was good, Ryan said, so good that he had an eye toward acquiring sixty acres across the road if he could convince his neighbor to part with them. He liked dealing with his present clients, the carriage trade. When they came to look over the ranch, they usually went away impressed and never asked how much anything cost.

"If they have to ask what it costs to board a horse," said Ryan, applying a layer of Chap Stick to his lips, then lighting up a Lucky, "you know they can't afford it."

Breeding season was just drawing to a close. It had begun in early February and would end promptly on the first of June. In season Ryan employed a crew of four to help him. He had three good stallions in residence, working studs who were booked up or nearly so. Each of them would cover about thirty-six mares before summer, sometimes two a day, one in the morning and one in the evening, and they were beginning to tire, as they did toward the end of every season, growing thin and edgy and mildly cantankerous. Ryan's ace stud was Fiddle Isle, who'd once stood at prestigious Claiborne Farm in Kentucky. Fiddle held the turf course record at a mile and a half at both Santa Anita and Hollywood Park and commanded a stud fee of twenty-five hundred dollars, insignificant by Kentucky standards but top-of-the-line in northern California. When he'd been turned out in 1970, his owners had syndicated him for a hundred thousand dollars. This meant the public could buy shares in his stud career just as they might back a comedy bound for Broadway. So far Fiddle hadn't paid much in dividends. It was possible he might close in Philadelphia. At thirteen he had more than a few crops behind him and he'd yet to sire a big winner. He didn't look very grand in his paddock. He'd lost about a hundred and fifty pounds since his racing days and his ribs were showing. He got along poorly with the other studs, and Ryan had had to put him in the barn, but he hated barns, too, and his ankles were scarred from kicking the walls. Now he had this paddock, a special enclosure in the shade of a live-oak tree. Ryan was annoyed about Fiddle's reputation as a sire. He felt the horse was being wrongly criticized. While it was true that Fiddle hadn't produced a star, his offspring tended to be strong and healthy and good on the turf. They were money-winners, Ryan said, which was more than you could say for the get of several studs whose reputations had been inflated by siring a single champion among many duds.

We stopped by a fenced pasture. Ten or twelve yearling colts were playing together, running from fence post to fence post in packs, nipping at each other and whinnying. They made an elegant sight with the blue sky and puffy cumulus clouds rolling out behind them. They ran and stopped, turning abruptly, and their legs, so delicate in relation to their upper bodies, seemed too frail to support them. The margin of error was slim. A chuckhole caught at the wrong angle could easily shatter a pastern, but the colts had to run. They were high-spirited and still a little wild. A score of pigeons and redwinged blackbirds flew around them, framing their beauty. "Have to get a shotgun pretty soon," Ryan said, eyeing the birds. I asked him if he ever became attached to the foals, and he said no, not really, this was a business.

"You just can't afford to do it. Some of these people, they say, 'Well, you can screw my wife and beat my kids, but don't you *ever* touch my horse.' That doesn't make any sense to me. Horses are dumb. They can kill you easy. Anything you get off a horse you're stealing."

"Can you tell much about these colts yet?"

Ryan nodded. "Usually with a yearling we can tell if he's going to be a runner. You can't say if he'll run in stakes, but you can be pretty sure he'll earn his keep. The good ones like to eat, they don't miss a meal, and they're aggressive."

Ryan didn't think much of Tesio. He'd read *Breeding the Racehorse* but it had given him no special insights. "You can read it in a couple hours," he said. "It's just a skinny little book." He had more respect for Rex Ellsworth, who worked with cheap stock but bred good horses, like Swaps. Most people didn't know what they were doing, Ryan said. They proceeded like hobbyists, without any practical experience in ranching or farming. They'd never spent any time around animals, so they romanticized horses and made mistakes. Trainers were not much help to the breeding industry either, not in Ryan's opinion. Often they owned studs, sometimes inferior ones, and they used their persuasive powers to attract business from the track, unsuspecting owners with mares in need of servicing. Trainers had too much sway, they were only in it for the money. The money wouldn't do them any good when they were dead, Ryan said. Besides, horses were difficult to breed, more difficult than cattle. It took five years to get through a generation of thoroughbreds, to see what you had, but with cattle it took only two. No matter what you were breeding, though, you were in for a heavy dose of the unpredictable. If you crossed a horse with a pony, you ought to end up with an animal this tall —Ryan marked a spot in the air midway between horse and pony size—but you didn't. And if you hit on something successful, a winning combination, you couldn't duplicate your result exactly, even if you covered the same mare with the same stallion in the same place at the same time of day in the same month with the moon in the same phase. Nothing was ever "the same"; it was hit or miss for sure.

"This isn't a particularly exciting business," Ryan said, "and it isn't particularly demanding. A friend of mine, a pilot, he used to say that flying consisted of long periods of boredom broken by moments of panic. Like when the red light goes on. That's what it's like around here."

I asked to see where the breeding was done, and he led me to an old barn, cool and dark and a little damp, with spider webbing in the rafters and baled hay piled high against the walls. I was surprised. The place I'd imagined was sterile and metallic, hi-tech, with aluminum surfaces and clamps and rods and the eerie lighting you see in hospitals and above the meat counter in supermarkets.

Ryan stood about ten yards inside the door, touching a spot on the floor with his boot. "This is it," he said. He could tell I was puzzled. "Nothing special. Just like any other barn." Even the mating itself sounded simple. A vet from Windsor examined the mares every two days, and when one of them went into estrus she was brought to the barn, washed down, and teased. The stud was usually ready to go. He sniffed around a bit and then mounted his partner, and then the mare was returned to her stall. The entire process, from wash-down to insemination, took about fifteen minutes. Ryan offered a live-foal guarantee, as did most breeders, and sometimes he had to cover a mare two or three times before she conceived. Maidens were the most trouble-some; with them he succeeded only sixty to seventy percent of the time. His biggest problem was recalcitrant mares who wouldn't stand still for the stud their owner had booked. They didn't un-derstand the business aspects of their predicament, the effort that had gone into correlating bloodlines, and so they kicked and fought and resisted as best they could. Ryan always managed to subdue them long enough for the studs to perform, but the semen was spent in service of a lost cause. The mares were resisting more deeply, all the way through, and only a few foals, said Ryan, were ever born of such unions.

Chapter Ten

The last week of Tanforan was marked for me by the creation of Emery's Angels. One day Bob Ferris disappeared, off to Longacres in his Exactamobile, and to replace him Emery hired the little blonde from the Home Stretch and her icy blond friend. They worked as grooms and confidantes, and Emery dressed them in crocus-yellow T-shirts emblazoned with the name of a new two-year-old filly of his, Fornofun. The Angels seemed happy around the barn and happier still in the paddock, especially the icy blonde, who was beautiful and seemed as she walked to draw a protective satisfaction from the horse she was leading. I was glad the Angels' wandering had ended at last. They would be cut loose soon, but in the meantime their position was secure, inviolable, and they moved around the backstretch with a newfound sense of authority. They were comfortable in the flux, drifting with the rest of us toward summer.

II

Bo Twinn's kittens were bigger now and still unclaimed, and as they crawled around over his lap they seemed an aspect of his condition rather than something he was likely to get rid of any time soon. He brushed them off distractedly, like a horse brushing away flies, and smoked a slow cigarette while sitting at the spool table reading his *Form*. His face was bathed in greenish light.

"Think she'll do it today, Bo?" I asked.

"I don't know," he said curtly. "I never know what she's going to do."

Pichi was entered in the sixth race. She was going up in class to sixteen thousand but dropping back to her preferred distance, six furlongs. Jimmy Colaneri's toothache was long gone and he'd be in the irons again, which meant she'd carry a hundred and nine pounds instead of the hundred and thirteen she'd carried under Mel Lewis. She had a chance, I thought, and nothing more.

"You come back here in an hour," Bo said, shooing me away. "Headley'll be here then with those people from Los Angeles."

"The Sandomirs?"

He made a disgusted face. "What other people is there who'd fly up from down south to watch *this* filly run?"

When I saw Headley go into the paddock after the fifth race I went down and joined him. He seemed nervous again, but he was more businesslike than usual and introduced me to Mary Sandomir, a small woman in blue. She was the sort of person who makes you feel good right away, putting you at your ease. Her hand was warm, and she smiled warmly and walked around the saddling stall with what might be called a purposeful dizziness, jumping from one thought or action to the next without much transition. She said her husband hadn't been able to make the trip, but she'd brought along her granddaughter Sandy and also two young friends of the family, Alan and his girl friend, both of whom wore Rolling-brand jeans. Mrs. Sandomir showed me her camera, then told Sandy, who was about seven, to stay close by because the men were bringing in the horses. When Bo led Pichi over, Mrs. Sandomir went right up to him. Her hair, rinsed with henna, almost matched Pichi's coat. Bo had done a bad job of shaving and his cheeks were spotted with blood, but this didn't prevent Mrs. Sandomir from giving him a little kiss and hugging him in a motherly way. I thought he'd sink into the bowels of the earth.

"How are you?" she asked. "You're looking good."

Bo looked at the dirt and muttered something unintelligible.

Mrs. Sandomir went closer to Pichi and rubbed her nose and the white blaze between her eyes, then stepped back and took her picture. She kissed the filly on the nose.

"Hello, baby," she said.

Bo led Pichi away. He seemed glad to be going.

"That horse," Mrs. Sandomir said, plucking at my shirt-sleeve, "she's so sweet. But she scares me. Oooh, she has such a temper!"

Jimmy Colaneri entered the paddock, tapping his boot with his whip. He was tall for a jockey, with long-lashed dark eyes and a polite manner that bespoke the ten years he'd put in waiting for a break. This was his first full season riding thoroughbreds—before he'd handled quarter horses—and so far it had been splendid. When he talked about his good fortune, he bubbled over and was capable of saying things like, "It just tickles me to death."

Mrs. Sandomir greeted him solicitously. "How you feel?" she asked.

"Aw, I'm fine," Colaneri said, blushing a little.

Mrs. Sandomir clucked through her teeth. "Last time his jaw was out to here," she said, holding her hand about ten inches from her jawbone to illustrate the extent of Colaneri's past misery.

Headley interrupted to give the jockey his instructions. He told Colaneri the strip was slow and reminded him to watch the early speed on either side of him in the gate.

"If you have to hit her, make sure you do it left-handed," he said. "I don't want her lugging in again."

Charlie Palmer, the paddock judge, called "Riders up," and Bo helped Colaneri into the saddle. Colaneri's red silks complemented Pichi's high chestnut color, and the filly moved forward with precision through the windswept air, her coat gleaming in iconographic tribute to the efforts of trainer and groom. For some reason the words from an old Grateful Dead song began churning in my brain:

> *Sometimes the light's all shining on me,*
> *Other times I can barely see.*
> *Lately it occurs to me*
> *What a long strange trip it's been.*

When I turned around, Headley was leaving for the grandstand. I wanted to go with him, but Mrs. Sandomir wanted to watch the race from the Owners' Pavilion, that tattered platform at the center of the paddock. This was a terrible vantage point. We could see the gate, but the entire backstretch was obscured by the toteboard and the horses wouldn't come back into our line of vision until they reached the stretch. Mrs. Sandomir was unconcerned. She scolded Alan for betting on the favorite, Andadora, then opened her purse and took out some photos. They were ordinary snapshots, the kind that feature children posed against a tree or jungle gym, but these were of horses, Pichi's relatives, a foal and another filly. The Sandomirs owned them both.

"We have a whole family," she said, "the two sisters and a baby."

The filly resembled Pichi, and I wondered if she could run. The odds were against it for sure. I had to admire the Sandomirs for intransigently following their hearts. Mrs. Sandomir waved the photos under my nose again, and I had the feeling she was about to tell me a great deal about the horses, foundation mares of a Sandomir dynasty, but then the gate opened and we were hooked by the flare-up of silks in the green metal mesh.

III

Later, Colaneri would remember a single moment from the race, when he'd opened his mouth to scream but nothing had come out. "I thought I was dead," he said. His troubles started in the gate when Pichi failed to respond to his urging. She broke poorly, trailing the field, and Colaneri was forced to rethink his strategy. He'd wanted to take her outside and run her there away from traffic and then make his move in the stretch, but now he was blocked ahead by a wall of flesh and couldn't maneuver in any direction. All he could do was sit tight and hope for a break. Seconds later he got one when a hole opened in the pack, a flash of daylight between horses. He touched Pichi with his whip and she came right on, making up ground. When she was almost to the hole, Mark Couto, the rider on Minnie B., turned around in his saddle and hit his mount hard. Colaneri recognized this as a habit of Couto's, something he did whenever his horse began to quit. Minnie B. slowed down a little anyway and drifted toward the center of the track, toward Jane Driggers on Silver Symmetry, and the hole began to close. Colaneri couldn't pull up on the reins, not without throwing Pichi dangerously off stride, and he couldn't move left or right, so he held on and kept driving and got caught in a pinch between horses.

Pichi was suspended between Minnie B. and Silver Symmetry. She ran as though she were in a vacuum, with just one foot touching the ground and the other three fanning the air. Neither Couto nor Driggers knew what was happening. They could feel the press of flesh, but because Colaneri hadn't screamed, they didn't know he was struggling for balance. Colaneri was thinking about his inevitable demise. When Pichi was released from the pinch, she'd land full force on one leg and the leg would break and down they'd go, horse and rider delivered to dust. Colaneri braced himself when Minnie B. pulled away, shutting his eyes against the impact. Then Pichi was free, a thousand pounds thrust down on a spindle of bone, but somehow her leg held together instead of exploding, and she planted another one after it, and another, righting herself without so much as a false step. Then she recovered her stride and continued, wholly redeemed, with nothing to lose. Colaneri couldn't believe it. He touched her again and took her outside, to see if she had anything left to give.

All this transpired in less than fifteen seconds, and when the horses disappeared behind the toteboard Pichi was running ninth, far back of Minnie B., who'd taken the lead. The next quarter mile was invisible to us, and the things around me took on a dreamlike quality. It was like being in a movie theater when the sound track suddenly cuts off. I became aware of my own breathing and the person breathing next to me, of life outside the frame. The platform seemed to wobble beneath my feet and I was hyperconscious of the fans in the grandstand behind me. I turned to look and saw them as molecules in a pattern, their bright shirts and blouses chromosomal beads. Mrs. Sandomir brought me back by touching my arm. She was very animated, disturbed by what she couldn't see, and she walked back and forth twisting a handkerchief between her fingers and asking the same question over and over again, "Where the hell is Pichi?" I think she wanted to be assured of a just outcome, but I had no such assurances to give. When the horses came into the stretch, I couldn't even find Pichi. But Alan could. He took Mrs. Sando-mir by the shoulders and pointed her in the right direction.

"Here she comes," he said. "She's on the outside."

Pichi made the most inelegant stretch run I'd ever seen. She went far too wide on the turn, awkwardly changing leads, but Colaneri spoke to her and she picked up the pace, passing horses at the back of the pack. She passed Breeze Ahead and Dancing Senorita and Pilfered Purse, all nags of little talent. For a minute it looked as if she would challenge the leaders, but when Colaneri hit her she lugged in. Colaneri was amazed. He was whipping her left-handed, just as Headley had told him to do, but instead of keeping her off the rail, the stroking seemed to be driving her toward it. Either she was rebelling against being hit or her inside bias was simply too strong to correct. The lugging was costing her dearly, she was losing ground. I folded my program in half and looked away, and then damned if she didn't start moving again, jump after jump, passing My Masai and drawing close to Minnie B. She gained another stride, and with fifty yards left pushed forward a little more and hooked Minnie B. head to head. Colaneri hit her and she jumped, and he hit her again at the wire, and she jumped again and seemed to pass through the photoelectric beam a split second ahead.

Immediately the PHOTO sign went up on the toteboard.

"Did she win?" asked Mrs. Sandomir.

"I think so," I said. "It looked like she got up on the last jump."

Alan thought she'd got up, too, and so did his girl friend, but none of us could be sure. It was a commonplace around the track that the camera saw things from a special angle, some point outside history, and the evidence captured on the photographic plate often diverged considerably from what you thought you'd observed. Horses materialized out of ectoplasm, and when you looked you saw *their* noses or heads touching the line, making a shambles of reality. So we waited silently for the verdict. Colaneri brought Pichi back, shook his whip at the stewards to let them know he had no complaints, and dismounted. Bo unstrapped the saddle and gave it to him, and he stepped onto the scales. I was watching Bo. A cigarette burned between his lips, and he led Pichi around in circles, cooling her out. If she won, his work would acquire a momentary significance. The care he'd lavished on her sore legs and sorry disposition would seem important, not just part of his job. You could tell him the care mattered even if she didn't win, but I don't think he would've believed it. He'd been on the backstretch too long and its singular sense of payoff was inculcated in him by now. But the matter was soon resolved, anyway. The photo tube came whistling down from the grandstand to the placing judges in the paddock, and the photo inside it showed clearly that Pichi had won. She had won by a neck and paid $18.80, and everybody on the platform went wild. Alan hugged his girl and said Gregory Sandomir would freak out when he heard the news, and the little girl Sandy ran from rail to rail participating in a joy she didn't quite understand. Tears rolled out from under Mary Sandomir's big sunglasses and down her cheeks, and she squeezed my arm tightly and wouldn't let go.

IV

After the race I went back to the barn to see how Pichi was reacting to her changed condition. She looked the same to me. She was on the hotwalker, going round, apparently indifferent, and Bo stood off to the side muttering to himself. He had his work clothes on again and was using a hose to water down the dust.

"Congratulations," I said.

"Well, she did it." A smile almost got him, but he ducked it just in time.

"She sure did."

"Yeah, she sure did do it."

"She looked terrific in the stretch."

"I thought she might do it but I wasn't sure. Colaneri, he give her a good ride."

"You know," I said, "that's the first time I didn't bet on her." Bo shut off the water. "I didn't bet on her, either."

"I was going to bet her. Hell, I was going to bet her across the board."

"I was going to bet her, too," Bo said, "but some son-of-a-bitch followed me to the window. They do that, some bastards, wait for you to come out of the paddock and see if you're going to bet. Everybody around here wants something for nothing."

I watched Pichi circling. Tesio said that horses left to their own devices will always walk a perfect circle, never an oval, because of the centers of balance in their ears.

"Well," Bo said, "I got all these stalls to clean." He moved inside and pulled the barn door closed behind him.

V

Much later that night I was sitting in the Home Stretch, high on Pichi's victory, staring at the mingled images of animals and humans on the back bar wall. Men and women with horses, horses with men and women. It had never struck me before how accurately the pictures reflected the composition of the backstretch. The proportions were almost exactly right, with the humans just slightly dominant. I remembered the recalcitrant mares of Windsor and I would've bet anybody in the joint that studs had some equally devious means of withholding their blessing, a technique for thinning out their sperm. Thoroughbreds were tricky, that much I had learned. They liked secrets, and even when boxed in and broken they retained a little wildness deep inside. Or maybe this was only their sixth sense, a few frames of *E. caballus* galloping across Mongolia spliced inextricably into the genetic film. They wouldn't run to form, no matter how you coaxed them, and in a world increasingly controlled and uniform this was exciting. When you picked a winner, especially at a price, you were buying back a little of your own wildness, cutting a wound into the smothering fabric of domesticity. We were starved, I thought, for contact with an animal other and experienced the lack as a form of sensory deprivation, a diminishment. The corporate fiction into which we'd fallen denied us our passions, and we were hurting because of it.

I had another bourbon and thought how thoroughbreds took us away. In their moment of running they had wings. When I was in touch with them, I felt the same way I felt on the river when I hooked a steelhead and it seemed to fire every neuron in my body, transforming me into one long synapse, bits of energy blowing apart. Why did fish so often strike your bait or fly when you were thinking about something else, lips, a bird, the moon, when you weren't "concentrating"? After the strike there was always a shock of recognition, learning again that water was a world, and of electricity, intercepting a charge in the flow. Whenever I beached a steelhead I looked at my line in wonder. It looked flimsy, and the knot attaching it to my hook was tiny and not very strong. *All connections ever tenuous.* I knew what was happening then. I was letting go of the sadness, letting go of my mother. Living and dying, winning and losing: I sat on the stool and drank my whiskey, suddenly permeated by all the emotions I'd been blocking out. Nothing abides; no cause for alarm.

Again I looked at the photos and thought how thoroughbreds resisted. In holding back that ounce of wildness they kept their dignity, and more than any quality of the flesh this made them beautiful. But I didn't know how long they could survive, not when faced with so many obstacles. In some sense our own survival was dependent on a continued mingling of the images, caring for what was sensate but inarticulate, or articulate only in ways we chose not to consider as speech. This was no way to end it, though, not after Pichi had made everything possible again, so I bought another bourbon and joined a groom down the bar who was talking to his *crème de menthe,* and together we discussed the horses and how great it was when one of them suddenly came alive and surprised everybody by winning a race.

VI

Pichi's win closed down my accounts. Of my initial five hundred dollars I had three hundred sixty-four dollars left. The seventh week was my undoing. Maybe the tactical changes I made (fewer bets but of greater magnitude, distributed among topflight trainers and stock) might have paid off over a longer period, but in the short run they proved devastating. I just couldn't accept the discipline imposed by such a limited scope. For five or six races, I'd sit tight, waiting for an opportunity to play, but if it didn't come I'd revert to the craziness of the first week and bet a large sum on an ill-considered filly and soon thereafter mark down a loss. I cashed a few tickets when I stayed within my self-imposed boundaries, but the truth was, win or lose, I didn't care any more. I was tired of the goddam *Form* and bored stiff with statistics. On the sixth of June I bought a newspaper and read the front page first. This was a signal event, the end of a flirtation.

Sometimes as I sat watching I wondered about the immemorial question of the track: Could the races be beaten? The answer was tough to swallow: Yes, they could be, but never by me. I lacked the qualities necessary for success—dedication to the profit motive, a high tolerance for the drudgery of daily handicapping and record-keeping, a cold, emotionless eye, a tightly controlled system, an accountant's approach to cash flow, and the cutthroat managerial attitude of a Harvard Business School grad. The few winners I knew weren't casual racegoers. More accurately, they worked for the track. Golden Gate Fields was their place of business and they reported every day because they couldn't get the edge they needed by hanging around a booking joint. They had to look over the horses personally, incorporate late scratches and jockey changes into their calculations, and keep tabs on the changing toteboard odds. Handicapping was their job, along with attending the races, and most of the time they enjoyed it no more than the average worker enjoyed his nine-to-fiver. And they were under considerable pressure, too; they earned no salary if they performed their job badly. Perhaps there were winners around for whom the excitement never died, but I'm sure they were in the minority. Besides, you could find blithe souls in any line of work, happy garbagemen, whistling dentists.

As for me, I was a loser, certainly not pleased with the label but not dismayed by it, either. The most important wager I'd made had paid off; the final cash outcome was not as significant. What I'd gotten from the track was pretty much what I'd deserved, conditioned in part by a desire to indulge in the precarious notion (a form of innocence? of losing?) that there was more to life than met the eye.

VII

That should be the end of my handicapping chronicle, but it isn't. Losers walking around with money in their pockets are always dangerous, not to be trusted. Some horse always reaches out and grabs them. In my case it was Plumb Dumb Bandit, sixth race, June 8, five furlongs on the turf. There was something about the way she looked, the *feeling* I got as she crossed over the main track and planted her hoofs confidently on the turf course. Confidently? How could I be falling into that trap again? On the other hand, how could the mare be going off at thirteen to one? She had three thirds in four starts, was five years old and Kentucky-bred; I was captured by the heartwarming suspicion that if her entire racing history were spread out before me, instead of just the most recent portion given in the *Form,* I'd discover in her past a victory or two on the grass. Yes, I was *convinced* she was a turf horse (anyone could see it), and I made my bet and watched her move confidently from seventh to first to take the race, winning by an indisputable length and returning $26.80. I won't say how much I collected, but it brought me close to even again, or maybe a little better, which meant, of course, that I had to make further bets to break the stalemate. The process is endless, I thought happily, endless.

VIII

On June 10, the last day of the meet, I left Golden Gate after the third race, drove directly to Spenger's, and took a seat in front of the wall-size TV to watch the Belmont Stakes. It seemed improbable that the race would be as good as the ones that had come before it, but it was, every bit as good, with Affirmed and Alydar hooked again, head to head all down the stretch, their movements, too, a kind of process, the margin between them so slim that the question of "winning" could not be resolved in any final sense. The day was Affirmed's once again, but ten minutes earlier or later it might have been Alydar's. The scale on which they had to be viewed invalidated the concept of competition; Michelangelo was not "better" than Leonardo.

After the race I couldn't pull myself away. I sat at the bar and watched the dinner crowd begin to fill the room, mostly Berkeley students who'd brought along parents or relatives in town for commencement. Everybody was on their best behavior, but little bouts of embarrassment surfaced here and there, a student wondered how his father had gotten so small or when his mother had become so foolish, and parents caught up in speculations about their children's sexuality and drug preferences.

About seven o'clock Jake Battles and some friends wandered in. They'd been celebrating the end of Tanforan somewhere else and they were extremely happy. As they settled in around a big circular table to wait for a table in the dining room, I cataloged the company in my notebook: Battles in his familiar red cardigan, his groom in a sport coat and cowboy hat, a ponygirl whose skin was chafed pink from six months of all-weather riding, a large puzzled woman in a heavy camel's hair coat, a young man dressed like a lumberjack, two pretty young women in thrift-shop glad rags, their cheeks rouged and flowery barrettes in their hair, and last, a stocky rubicund man who kept running back and forth to the oyster bar and depositing plates of oysters and clams on the table. His offerings were ignored. The oysters just sat there being luminescent. In a while "Battles, party of eight," came over the loudspeaker, but nobody at the table responded, nor did they move when the call was repeated five minutes later. The third time I heard it, I finished my bourbon and went out the door.

IX

The summer was hot and dry, as it always is where I live, and the winter rains came late. The fishing was terrible. Old-timers said it was the worst season they could remember. I caught only two steelhead and one of them, a little male, was spent and bright red. When people asked me why the fishing was so bad, I told them the steelhead could feel the dam being built, and with it the message of extinction, although there were more realistic factors involved, including high muddy water and some voracious sea lions at the river mouth.

Golden Gate opened in late January, and I followed the action from a distance. Management had renovated the racing strip, banking it in accordance with the 1947 blueprints and blending in top sand, redwood sawdust, and mushroom compost to give it bounce, but it wasn't holding up well under the rains. Two of the finest horses on the grounds, Captain Don and Boy Tike, broke down, and one morning eleven two-year-olds working in company slipped and fell in the mud. Halfway through the meet there was a stupendous accident right in the middle of the strip, with horses sprawled flat and two riders thrown and almost killed. The footage was so graphic that Bay Area TV stations showed it on both evening and late news programs. When horsemen refused to race the next day, the Pacific Association closed down for twenty-four hours to make the necessary repairs.

The Tanforan Association fared no better. Though the rains had stopped by April, pari-mutuel clerks went on strike when automatic ticket-selling equipment was introduced into the pari-mutuels department, costing the union some jobs. Management hired scabs to replace them, but fans were reluctant to cross the picket lines and instead took in the quarter-horse races at Bay Meadows. Attendance dropped radically, down by almost fifty percent. When the clerks signed a new contract and returned to work in mid-May, the association tried to recoup some of its losses by cutting back on the size of purses being awarded, lopping three thousand dollars from an allowance race, twenty thousand for a handicap. Everybody felt the pinch, and during the last third of the meet, thousand-dollar exactas were as common as pollen in the breeze.

X

But in accordance with Tesio's law, I was feeling better, restored if not renewed. I borrowed a device from the shield Lorenzo had carried in his betrothal ceremony, that of a bay tree half dead, half green, pictured above the motto, *The spring returns.* It was a good spring, too, rich with promise. In my mind the dying and the cancer had become separated, almost discrete, the one a natural process of organic decay, the other a cultural hastening of that process. Resistance was the key, holding on to the model, the waves of the brain reaching out like the legs of a Devonian creature scrambling up from the sea and onto the land. Slow determined extensions toward prosperity in the human heart; what was any renaissance but a sudden bias in favor of hope?

Souvenirs of Golden Gate were scattered around the trailer, wads of losing tickets, cardboard boxes full of *Forms*, a few photos of horses and jockeys. Ted's globe rested on a table, intransigently circumscribed. I thought what a paltry representation it made of what we knew. Walter Pater once said of Pico's world that it was "bounded by actual crystal walls, and a material firmament; it was like a painted toy," and I could hear if I tried the sound of the walls being shattered, by Columbus first, then Copernicus. But the walls were always being shattered, breaking open here and there, the globe mapped and remapped. More often than ever I was happy just to ford the river and climb the hills of the sheep ranch. Someday the model would obtain, the dam would silt up, the cardboard houses would be blown away, and the steelhead would return to the river in great numbers, or to another river of equal importance. Whether or not I saw them return no longer concerned me. They would return. Just this then, to make every world the New World, to approach it with an explorer's sense of wonder.

At ten o'clock I arrived here at this *Cape del Isleo* and anchored, as did the caravels. After having eaten, I went ashore, and there was there no village but only a single house, in which I found no one, so that I believe that they had fled in terror, because in the house were all their household goods. I allowed nothing to be touched, but only went with these captains and people to examine the island. If the others, which have been already seen, are very lovely and green and fertile, this is much more so, and has large and very green trees. There are here very extensive lagoons, and by them and around them are wonderful woods, and here and in the whole island all is as green and the vegetation is as that of Andalusia in April. The singing of little birds is such that it seems that a man could never wish to leave this place; the flocks of parrots darken the sun . . .

—Christopher Columbus
October 21, 1492

Afterword

I read several books during my stay at the Terrace, and a few, other than those mentioned in the text, proved especially useful: *Horizon* magazine's *Lorenzo de' Medici and the Renaissance,* the National Geographic Society's *The Renaissance, Maker of Modern Man,* McGraw-Hill's *The Age of the Renaissance,* and Lucas-Dubreton's *Daily Life in the Time of the Medici* provided excellent background material; Michael Levey's *High Renaissance* started me thinking about Cellini's saltcellar; Donald Weinstein's *Savonarola and Florence* led me away from a more traditional interpretation of the friar's life; Josephine Burroughs's essay on Ficino and Paul Oskar Kristeller's on Pico (both in Cassirer, Kristeller, and Randall's *The Renaissance Philosophy of Man*) contributed to my understanding of those writers' works; and Francis Yates's *Giordano Bruno and the Hermetic Tradition* and D. P. Walker's *Spiritual and Demonic Magic: From Ficino to Campanella* gave me a firm grounding in my approach to Renaissance magic.

Three books among the many I read about horses and racing should also be cited: Donald Braider's *The Life, History and Magic of the Horse,* Roger Longrigg's *The History of Horse*

Racing, and Zarn, Heller, and Collins's book/pamphlet "Wild, Free-Roaming Horses—Status of Present Knowledge," published by the Department of the Interior. I learned about Albany's history from the Police and Fire Employees' Civil Service Club's *The Story of the City of Albany,* and about Costonoans from Alfred Kroeber's work and also from Charles Bohakel's *Indians of Contra Costa County.* The press and media guides published annually by Golden Gate Fields told me what I needed to know about the track.

I owe thanks to Golden Gate's Clifford Goodrich for granting me access; Ellen Burnett, former racing secretary, for answering questions and digging up statistical matter; Gene Brucker, University of California, for advice on and criticism of my reading of the Renaissance; Amanda Vaill, for her editorial enthusiasm and skill; and Elaine Markson for her long-standing commitment.

Although this is a book of nonfiction, I have in two or three places invented names for people who slipped by too fast to be pinned down, or who for other reasons deserve their anonymity.

II

A final note on the flux: The Home Stretch has changed ownership and many of the memorabilia formerly on display have disappeared; the dam, Warm Springs in Sonoma County, is nearing completion; and the management at Golden Gate, after losing over a million dollars in 1979, has hired a consultant to redesign the racing strip and a new track superintendent to maintain it.

Photo by David Timmons

ABOUT THE AUTHOR

Bill Barich is the author of ten books of fiction and non-fiction. Amazon lists *Laughing in the Hills* among its ten best sports book of the twentieth century, while *Sports Illustrated* calls it one of the 100 best of all time. He has been a Guggenheim Fellow, a frequent contributor to *The New Yorker*, and a literary laureate of the San Francisco Public Library, having lived in the Bay Area for many years before moving to Dublin.